# American Vacation

# AMERICAN VACATION

12,000 Miles Into the Wild West

Raluca Barbu

First eBook edition published in Romanian in April 2020
Romanian title: Vacanță americană. 20.000 de km în vestul sălbatic

Translation: Raluca Barbu, Aurora Moldovan
Adaptation and editing: Christina Roemer-Goldstein, Danell Montgomery Waters, and Richard Lynas
Cover photo: Mihai Ciornei
Layout: Raluca Barbu
Inserted photographs by Mihai Ciornei and Raluca Barbu

# CONTENTS

*To M.*

# SPECIAL THANKS

**M**. and I are two people whose lives entwined at an age when unpredictability is an unlikely encounter in the story. When the future seems to be already laid out. To our surprise, and contrary to this conviction, this age could also be a time when the most fantastic events occur. It happened to us. Only something out of the ordinary has the power to uproot old beliefs about ourselves and our union is a perfect depiction of this theory. Us meeting and starting a life together is the far-fetched element of the narrative while our American vacation is proof of how unforeseeable life really is.

We are very different, having carried distinct spiritual luggage for several decades, each of us in corners of the world that have nothing in common. However, we have been lucky enough to start with a clean slate, discovering new worlds in one another. M.'s world has mountains, deserts, woods, and oceans tied together by the yearning of being among them. Mine is a world of words and stories eager to be written.

Together with this journey, I received from M. his love and dedication. I learned from him that a genuine bond between people goes beyond money, expectations, or time. I witnessed firsthand that true love for nature means sharing it as well. It was my honor to be the one with whom M. shared it. Being with him, I found a new self on the trails of the Wild West, and a new love that brought me a kind of happiness I never knew existed. A happiness I didn't expect to deserve.

In a way, I too became wild and therefore understood nature, camouflaging in its midst and feeling its pulse. The time spent together on a mountaintop, on the ocean shore, in the middle of the desert, or on a volcano brim was so generously offered to me. He wanted to share with me his favorite places, his history. He'd said he would and he did just so.

I did my best to keep up with him or better said he slowed down to my pace, and encouraged me to go forward no matter what. I shared his enthusiasm, and he always found new ways to elicit my admiration, not for the challenge itself, but for translating his reverence to nature. While I became more familiar with the world, our bond grew stronger. We now can communicate in Romanian, English and Wild.

# PROLOGUE

*" We do not take a trip; a trip takes us."*[1]

T his book exists because of two reasons: a trip and the revelation that a month and a half is not a regular amount of time for one. It had been a fantasy that became the reality of my summer in 2018, under circumstances known only by M. You just cannot cram forty-five days into a conversation among friends, as I discovered after a few failed attempts, nor into a traveler's blog post that would inform its occasional readers. This amount of time accumulates so much more than a number of miles, and tourist attractions and, therefore, deserves a lot more attention. And space.

This is why, being a writer, I came to the obvious conclusion that celebrating the beauty of one-third of the American territory deserves at least a few hundred pages of well-crafted paragraphs gathered between spectacular covers. It would be the perfect place for all the spontaneous elements of our travel: the people, and the animals that we encountered, and most of all, the places that had needed hundreds of millions of years to develop the flawless gorgeousness that they exhibit today.

After subtracting everything countable, I remain with the acquaintances I made on the top of a mountain, or admiring a spectacular waterfall; with an entire array of feelings that excited me while discovering how spellbinding nature is; with everything that it bequeathed me; with the amazement of how ingenious and surprising human nature is. In the end, it is me and my discoveries, the obstacles that I overcame and the knowledge that nobody could have ever taught me

Whenever you find me staring out into space with the corners of my mouth shaping a perfect smile, I might be off to a desert patch where a chipmunk, up on its hind legs, is begging for a piece of my apple. It often happens that I recollect sequences of my North-American vacation. And I can't help it. First, because I still find it impossible to have occurred; then, admitting its reality. After all, I squeezed an excessive amount of life into the ephemerality of forty-five days. I would revisit those memories repeatedly until the time invested in the process would dilute the concentration of the vacation.

After our return I gathered all the notes from my logbook, all the people, the animals, the plants, the weather, the landforms, the food, the highs, the lows, the enthusiasm, the exhaustion, M. and me, as we were exploring together along vast areas of the United States of America, and created a travel book without precedent.

☼

You are about to read a story about a nature journey, through the West in the summer — just so you know what is in store for you. There are no chapters about shopping in New York, hotels in Las Vegas, or Michelin star restaurants in Miami. Although we wander along most of the Western coast, many times side by side with the Pacific Ocean, we do not get to Los Angeles and do not run into any movie stars. That is not the theme of this excursion. Instead, we reach the northernmost point of the United States, Cape Flattery, where the Makah tribe still live and where, at least in theory, one would be able to see Canadian ground. If the fog did not have the consistency of buttermilk.

Technically, M. and I are the lead characters of this tale, but we are rather the beneficiaries of the experiences we purposely or accidentally walked into. The main protagonists are the people with whom we exchange a few words, the animals, which are peacefully foraging as we are passing through their dwelling places, and all the landforms that I did not even know existed before I made their acquaintance, starting with their exotic names: *canyon, gulch, tufa, hoodoo, arch*, etc.

The apparel is casual/hiking/sport, washed weekly at the laundromat of whatever hotel we happen to spend the night. The shoes are dusty, directly proportional to the hundreds of hiked miles. At one point, I start believing that I have outgrown my shoes, or that maybe my feet have swollen because of the heat. In fact, my shoes are just full of sand of various colors. Only the first photos we took show their original color.

The sunglasses had become part of our faces as we can count less than a dozen days when the sun was not flamingly caressing our heads, and we did not have to take shelter under their tinted lenses. The facial tan has a strap pattern towards the temples and the skin has its former tone only between the eyebrows and cheekbones.

The means of transportation is a rented all-wheel-drive SUV M. specifically chose to help us face all of the winding roads mentioned in his spreadsheet that sum up our vacation. It is comfortable and roomy enough to carry the two of us in the front seats, and a cooler filled to the brim with fruit, ice, water, and beer bottles in the back seat. In the trunk, we have two suitcases with our all-season clothes, tent, sleeping bags, folding chairs, and crunchable snacks.

Ninety-nine percent of the 12,250 miles we are about to leave behind are paved, properly marked, and amazingly maintained at sea level or 6,000-foot altitudes, such as interstates, highways, and routes. The all-wheel-drive will be vital to us one percent of the time, when we are in the Vermilion Cliffs, Arizona, on our way to the White Pocket and a second time reaching 9,000 feet towards Mount White, where the roads are sandy and rocky.

Distances pile up in miles and my mind has to do the math multiplying one mile by 1.6 so that I can understand how many kilometers we are talking about. It makes no difference while we are driving, because I just sit in the passenger seat, admiring the scenery, reading, or writing down in detail what we do each day. But while on the trail, it's not the same mentally if there are seven miles left, (which means eleven kilometers), or as it happened on Mount White when there were nineteen miles left (which meant thirty kilometers). Numbers seem to have a strong impact on my brain.

Time passes here the same as back home in Romania, where I am originally from, but I constantly have to add seven to ten hours to the clock, depending on where we are, to make sure it is a reasonable time to call my family. When we reach the Pacific

Coast, it is the easiest, as we go to bed when they wake up and vice versa.

Most of my expectations turn out to be preconceived. It is no wonder since my only sources of inspiration were American movies and TV shows. None of the things I have imagined America would represent turns out to be true, and the examples are endless.

Ever since M. started planning this vacation, close to a year ago, he has been fascinatingly and impatiently telling me about the Sonoran Desert. All I could imagine were dunes, drought, and unbearable heat. After crossing it almost entirely, I discovered that it stands at high altitude, that it is not flat, that the Colorado River waters its thirsty land, and that the least believable thing of all is that it can snow in the winter over the Sonoran Desert.

Just to give you an example of my ignorance: I knew that halfway into our journey we would reach the Pacific Coast. All I could expect in my tourist mind were sunny days, hot sandy beaches, invigorating waves, swimming suits, and enviable Baywatch tans. M. warned me that reality will contradict my expectations, but I never imagined myself shivering on most of the beaches in California, Oregon, and Washington, or that I would be dressing up to my teeth in a windbreaker, with the same scarf I imagined wearing over the bathing suit but tightly wrapped around my neck instead. On the western shore of the United States the cold, the wind, and the fog coexist in perfect harmony with the blue of the sky and the ocean. The fantasies about tanning and drinking rainbow-colored umbrella cocktails seem to happen elsewhere. Not there.

Another unexpected fact I came across while traveling from Texas to New Mexico and Arizona, driving through dusty small towns with commanding names like Van Horn, El Paso, and Las Cruces, places where I barely heard English, is that this entire area was a Mexican territory at some point in history. To be more exact, the states of California, Nevada, Utah, most of Arizona, half of New Mexico, a quarter of Colorado, and a bit of Wyoming once belonged to Mexico.

Don't misjudge me. I feel I should explain myself. Clearly, I could have learned any of these things by just googling them. At least. But I waited for the trip to materialize and then to learn all the facts on the spot because, to be honest, I did not believe this vacation would materialize until the plane took off from London to Chicago. To be even more honest, there were still quite a few other moments, while finding myself in the middle of M.'s thoroughly crafted itinerary, when I didn't believe that I was the one living them. Anyway, we all have some fears and anxieties that prevent us from believing that we deserve the beautiful things happening to us. The thought of some of us being united in this sense gives me a lot of relief.

I was born and bred in Romania. Most of my experiences have occurred on Romanian soil, in a Romanian style. Therefore, everything I witness somewhere else I automatically compare to what is familiar to me. The bigger the difference or contradiction, the more complex my emotions are likely to be. Visiting the Western Continental States was one of those empirical trials, elaborate and profoundly different from anything I have seen before in my country. Or Europe, for that matter. What I take with me from all the awe and appreciation is exactly what makes this trip memorable. Specifically what is so radically different from Romania.

I do not intend to compare or ask rhetorical questions like, *"Why is it possible somewhere else?"* because the answers dig deep into the history and mentality of a nation.

All I aim to do is tell you about a distinct world, unlike the one I presumed it was, about people and the way they relate to one another, about places where nature concentrated a dizzyingly amount of beauty and wilderness, and about the care and respect the locals and tourists have for this heritage.

# CHAPTER I - *ILLINOIS, THE LAND OF LINCOLN* ☼ *MISSOURI, THE SHOW-ME STATE*

# 1 - *SPRINGFIELD, IL ☼ ST. LOUIS, THE DEVIL'S ELBOW, SPRINGFIELD, MO*

The joyride begins on a certain Thursday in June, in Gilberts, Illinois. We start in a silver-green Subaru Forester, early in the morning, when the sky has not yet cleared its forehead, and we cannot tell for sure if it is frowning at us or just still dozing. After a few tens of miles, it becomes obvious. It starts pouring rain as if to clean the road before us and to smooth it for the thousands of miles that we are about to drive. First South, West, North, and then back East until we return to where we started, creating a geometrical shape that will hopefully gain a name by the end of the trip.

First, we cross suburbs where the architecture of the houses compliments the landscape, with open lawns and no fences, freshly mowed grass, clumps of trees that frame the houses with shade and breeze, and two rocking chairs on the front porch.

We are on Illinois State Routes 47 and 64, where I can easily admire the typical suburban scenery where many Americans choose to live, away from the busy urban areas. I would choose the same scenery if it were the case, despite the cold winters. If I were to find a Romanian equivalent of these small towns, it would have to be the countryside. But it would only be by name, because there aren't any roosters cock-a-doodle-doo-ing at dusk or dogs barking, and there aren't any clothes hung up to dry in the yards, no coops, no vegetable beds, no burning garbage heaps, no old ladies sitting on benches by the side of the road. It rather looks like residential areas, where houses are reasonably far from one another, all showing off colorful flower beds, pools, and trampolines.

The sky rinses and the sun shows up in a corner of the windshield right when we enter Interstate 39. Just then, I discovered the sunroof our vehicle possesses with such pride. I will take advantage of it quite a few times. When passing through the redwood forests in California I look up at their dizzying height;

I climb out of it up to my waist to photograph the bison herds in Hayden Valley in Yellowstone, Wyoming; and coming back to Illinois we are welcomed back by the same rain as today, tapping furiously on the same sunroof.

With the Interstate under the wheels, endless before us, the first thing that strongly affects me is the vastness of the space and horizon. Everything is so large in comparison with Europe that it all seems to be enormous, colossal, and gigantic. Yes, all the synonyms. As I will discover later on, in this country everything is big: houses, cars, malls, roads, lakes, washing machines, marshmallow bags, or portions of fries. Somehow, this is the key feature of all that is American.

After 326 miles and a quick stop in Springfield, the capital of Illinois, we reach St. Louis, one of the biggest cities in Missouri. Our trip is not about this kind of sightseeing, but whenever we have the chance to look at the skyline of a city from a distance, we do so.

Here we are, admiring St. Louis over the Mississippi River. Unlike Europe, all the large cities in the United States have a skyline, meaning a specific print against the horizon, following the outline of the downtown. The connoisseurs can easily identify any city by this outline. From afar, we get to take pictures of The Gateway Arch in all its steel glory. Its 630-foot height makes it the tallest arch in the world and the tallest monument built by man in the Western hemisphere.

Coincidentally, we passed by the arch on the same day as a good friend of ours, just a few hours apart and in opposite directions. This will happen to us again with another friend as we leave San Francisco and figure out that we have been admiring each other's photos of the same places on Facebook, but taken one day apart. We do not get a chance to see any familiar faces on our trip, but we get to make new wonderful acquaintances.

After a healthy lunch at Whole Foods, and a quick view of the Busch Baseball Stadium, the house of the St. Louis Cardinals (eleven-time champions so far), we get on Interstate 44. As soon as we leave Newburg behind, we take the notorious Route 66, driving parallel to the interstate on one side and with a lush wooded area on the other. Orange wild lilies spot the curbs, and milky steam comes out of the asphalt, probably an effect of the morning rain.

Around mile 490, we arrive at The Devil's Elbow, a lesser-known tourist attraction, but picturesque and secluded. One can admire the Big Piney River as it bends just like an elbow, giving the same shape to the Fort Leonard Wood that encloses it. This is where we notice turtles swimming freely, the first on the long list of wild animals going around doing their business in this country. We photograph them with the same intensity as we do the Route 66 signs. You can find them on the side of the road (the signs, I mean, not the turtles), on the pavement, and artistically scratched on the bark of a tree that stands as a totem for the nearby restaurant.

It would be less of an authentic American day if we were not already on the famous Route 66. Along the 2,500 miles from Illinois to California, crossing eight states, it seldom runs parallel to the interstate. They preserve it as a scenic route precisely for allowing the travelers to witness the beauty and specificity of the American geography, which would be less obvious from the monotonous interstate. Throughout the 12,250 miles of our trip, we drive several times on Route 66, and each time I feel equally enthusiastic.

We spent the night in Springfield, Missouri, at the Quality Inn, in room 205, at mile number 585.

Interestingly, there are around fifty cities in the USA named Springfield, almost one for each state, and we drive through two of them on the same day. This first night I start a long list of things I forget in hotel or motel rooms, campgrounds, and lodges.

# CHAPTER II –

## *ARKANSAS, THE NATURAL STATE* ☼ *OKLAHOMA, THE SOONER STATE*

# 2 - *OZARK NATIONAL FOREST, WHITAKER POINT, AR* ☼ *GEORGETOWN, TX*

R oute MO65 gets us out of Missouri, and then AR43 welcomes us into Arkansas under impeccable weather. We go up and down on wooded hills, not leaving any angle of the countryside undiscovered until we reach Ozark National Forest, where our first trail awaits. The day presents us with a green and orange hot-air balloon that flies through the sky. Across the highway, there is a yard with broccoli-like trees, and as far as you can see there are cows, goats, and horses animating the landscape. No wonder, since both states are entirely covered in fresh green that is perfect for grazing.

The day becomes even more eccentric when we spot a fully decorated Christmas tree by the side of the road. This will not be the only one we encounter along the way, because somewhere in California we speed by another one.

After mile 676, we enter a two-way road with the Buffalo River accompanying us on one side. The kayak shop we stop at shortly after confirms this is a recreational area. We find ourselves at the first trailhead of our journey twenty miles down the road. The first of sixty-five.

Every trailhead we see looks identical to the next one, no matter the state, park, altitude, or relief. Their purpose is to mark the beginning of the trail, to inform the hikers about its length, difficulty, and duration of the walk, and how much water you need to avoid dehydration. Most of them display a panel with a map of the attraction and the available trails (the Ozark National Forest alone offers over 370 miles of trails) magnified in the geographical area. The moment you leave the trailhead behind, you agree to keep your steps inside the trail at all times back and forth.

Americans care deeply for their nature. One reason these trails are so firmly defined before being put to use is that they invite the hikers to enjoy the walk and then leave nature intact afterward. Therefore, our experience in all the parks is quite authentic, because it feels like visiting the house of nature and animals, where only the footprints of the boots can prove the presence of humans. There is no garbage on the side of the trail, no empty rusted cans pushed into hollows, no plastic bags hanging from tree branches, no toilet paper or wet wipes left to biodegrade in glades, no makeshift fireplace used for grilling sausages as it happens in my country. Unfortunately. The American authorities do everything decently and thoughtfully, including placing ecological toilets at every trailhead, supplied with toilet paper and hand sanitizer. There are plenty of trash bins everywhere and even recycling bins in crowded tourist areas. All is done for the guests, nature, and my pure amazement that something like this exists.

Whitaker Point is our first incredible hiking destination, more for me than for M., who has been here before quite a few times. The spot itself is a crag coming out of the mountain and stands still over a glen that goes on up to the horizon, with green plaids of pine and oak timber. I am almost dizzy finding myself suspended under an impeccable azure sky and over the raw green of Arkansas.

If we were to come here during a rainy autumn or an early spring when the snows are melting, we would find a few spectacular waterfalls on the way up, but that is not the case amid this torrid summer. M. was lucky enough to see them every time he hiked this trail, right when spring gave in to summer, which makes me think of global warming that appears to be more and more real.

On our way up, we encountered a couple of deer, a woodpecker, a hawk, and a snake. As usual, whenever we cross paths with wildlife, we stare, take pictures and videos, and startle at their every move, as if we have just received the most unusual guests and not the other way around.

I am not that fortunate to get to cool under the natural shower of a waterfall but I get a different treat. When we reached the summit of our hike, a group of women wearing long dresses with several layers and white bonnets on their heads seemed to have just woken up. They appear to have camped here overnight and slept in hammocks right on the brim of the rock. I don't get to examine their appearance or listen to them talking for long enough, but the hazard of meeting them is exotic to me, unusual as a trip to the past, in the time of the first pioneers. America unveils itself to me in its entire splendor, as a land with living history.

Leaving behind the feminine religious cult and 790 miles, we are off to Texas, crossing the Western corner of Oklahoma on the way. Every state has its slogan, in fact some have several, and they call this one *Native America* or *The Sooner State*. It is also called America of the Native People, because in the 20th-century one-third of the Cherokee tribe was moved here. And *The State of the Hurried Ones* because when the first colonists arrived here, some of them weren't patient enough to wait for the kick-start and cheated by occupying the richest lands before everyone else.

America is still in a way the land of cowboys and Indians, and I have to admit I never stopped to think about what this meant. I have an opportunity to do so right now, crossing vast territories where Native Americans were exiled. My knowledge of these people is limited to the western movies I used to watch as a child, so everything I know has cinephile origins.

We drive through Oklahoma and the Cherokee Nation; in Arizona, and the Navajo Nation; in New Mexico and the Zuni and Pueblo People; in Washington and the Makah Indian Reservation. What I learn about them is that they have their own government, like a state within a state, living by their own laws. They are poor and their towns show it. They occupy sizable areas of the desert that include several extremely popular tourist attractions, such as Monument Valley, Antelope Canyon, and Horseshoe Bend, but this changes nothing in the way they have to live their lives. With all this in mind, we drive by their houses with rocking chairs on the porch and big yellow flowers planted in front, and graveyards embellished with shrill colored artificial flowers.

We stop for lunch not in an American place, nor a Native

American one, but at Cabana Mexican Restaurant, where we have delicious camarones[2] wrapped in bacon, with guacamole, salad, rice, beans, and tortillas. As usual, the portions are huge and we have to take half of them to eat the next day for breakfast. It says *Mexelent* food on the restaurant's window, and I agree.

After almost 1,000 miles, we enter Texan territory and a new climate, humid and hot. From now on, the temperatures will not go under 100–110 Fahrenheit.

We drove by Dallas listening to the soundtrack of the TV show with the homonym name, and then by Austin. Both cities follow the American standard of hugeness. It takes close to 3 hours to drive around them. We watch the Dallas skyline in the generous dusk light and Austin's in plain darkness, which is why our photos immortalize only the sparkles dotted by the skyscrapers into the Colorado River.

I take the splendor of this night with me and fall asleep thinking of JR and Sue-Ellen in the Fairfield Inn, Georgetown, Texas, room 235.

# CHAPTER III - *TEXAS, THE LONE STAR STATE* ☼ *NEW MEXICO, LAND OF ENCHANTMENT*

# 3 - *PEDERNALES FALLS STATE PARK, THE ENCHANTED ROCK STATE NATURAL AREA, SOUTH LLANO RIVER STATE PARK, JUNCTION, TX*

A t mile 1,329, we check the first state park off our list. Pedernales Falls State Park, Texas. It is a wonder of a park, a piece of heaven, a corner of the world that I would happily return to any time. To be fair, it is only the first one I am visiting and this might be the reason I am so impressed with it, but I don't expect that my level of enthusiasm would drop if it were the last one on the list.

All the recreational activities happen around the Pedernales River, over a thirteen-mile area, and they manifest in all the aquatic forms that a river can offer. Supposedly, the limestone riverbed is 300 million years old. In some parts, it runs smoothly between sandy shores and old artisanal trees—this is where the swimming area is. In other parts, it gets agitated and speeds up because of the chute—this is the tubing area. In some places, the waters are calm and deep—this is the fishing area. Moreover, there are vast spaces of limestone slabs shaped in creative forms that the river sculpted over millions of years, where the water is only ankle deep. During the wet seasons, these areas are flooded and emerald green ponds form everywhere.

Tens of hiking, biking, and horseback riding trails and camp-grounds map out the hills and valleys that the river runs among writing in calligraphy known only by it. It is also the perfect spot for geocaching or bird watching. Theoretically, any river in the world could offer the possibility of a good time, but this is the first place I am finding the whole concept put into practice with such skill.

This place mesmerizes me, with the emerald green shade that the limestone gives to the water where it is shallow. I am surprised with the shells scattered on the riverbanks and with the first cactus bushes I see in my life. There are deer dressed in velvet brown grazing in clearings, green lizards so fast we can hardly follow with our eyes, and two opposing groups of enthusiastic Asian tourists competing in a team-building game. Everything is full of life and color here, but what has a powerful impact on me is how clean and well managed this park is.

The National Park Service—U.S. Department of the Interior - administrates fifty-eight national parks, and we get to visit thirty-three this summer. What attracts me in this first park replicates again thirty-two more times, with slight differences given by their size and number of visitors.

The Park entrances are all in the shape of a ranger's cottage, strategically placed in the middle of the road, to have access to both coming and leaving guests. The staff are all dressed in olive drab uniforms and wide-brimmed hats. They check your pass or sell you a ticket as you drive in. Then, they offer you a map of the park and a flyer with all the amenities available on-site and all the open trails. Some parks have a newspaper with articles about the park's history, benefactors, restorations, flora, and fauna. They have a schedule for park-related activities and classes that the rangers and staff offer to the kids or adults throughout the summer on wildlife, geology, and astrology. Sometimes, they organize star gazing nights in their amphitheater. The staff is polite, smiling, and enthusiastically welcoming, always there to answer questions. They say *"Welcome"* and *"Have a nice day"* to every visitor!

Before lacing up your hiking boots and strolling on the trails, you first make a stop at the Visitor Center. It's a must. They come in all sizes, with a few employees or tens of them. The buildings can be quite small or imposing two-story structures. Most of them exhibit a scale model of the park and surrounding areas so that the visitors can learn the geography of the place in its entirety. Numerous informative flyers are available so that any trip to the Visitor Center can be a real lesson if you have an open mind. Here is where you find out about the snow melting on the high-altitude trails or the flooding of the river and which of the trails are open for pets.

Inside there is usually a souvenir shop, sometimes a bookstore, and a restaurant. All of them have a designated area for the boy and girl scouts and sell postcards you can stamp with the park name and date. Some of them have museums inside, displaying rocks and fossils, or photographs and paintings of the park. In any of them, you can refill your water bottle and use the restrooms. In two of them, I even get to buy earrings.

I keep telling M. how unusual this form of tourism seems to me, one that allows you to visit a natural reservation, and that provides all the needed information and support of trained staff. By the time you have to leave you have learned so many facts about the place and also have had a good time. M. always answers me in the same way. This is not unusual, but normal. However, for me, coming from another country, all of this is exceptional.

Around the lunch hour, when the car display shows 111°F and 1,396 miles into the trip, we reach the Enchanted Rock State Natural Area, a half-sphere-shaped mountain the Tonkawa tribe used to consider magical. The one-mile hike to the summit seems to expand with every step we take. Our boot soles stick to the rock as we climb as if melting when in contact with the hot surface, and the sun appears to increase the gravitational force with no reason at all.

Going up, I feel my pulse growing alarmingly after every twenty steps, and my cheeks burn as if I have a fever. The sweat is even hotter than the air I breathe if possible. This is how I conclude, with my now melted analytical abilities, what all the hikes will be like in the desert. I am grateful for not succumbing to heat and humidity, because I get to see what lies at the bottom of the mountain in all compass directions.

In a perfect circle, under a globe of blue sky, the horizon gathers within its borders the first desert I see in my life. All around, there are spiky shrubs and isolated small ponds of a condensed green color that stay wet only because of the magic of the mountain.

Up there, I understand the irresistible power of The Enchanted Rock. Although entirely exposed to the sky and fully visible from all around the mountain - except for the foothill -

I feel safe, above everybody and everything. On this rock, that stands directly under the magnifying glass of the sun, with no shade or protection, the cacti are alive, pulpy, and broiling. I touch them and absorb their energy. I see many hollows filled with boiling water on the surface of the mountain and cannot understand how it does not evaporate, considering that it only rains a few times a year in these parts. Just as strange, I find the existence of animals on this hot stove. A squirrel jumps from under the shade of a cactus to another, and its tiny paws would burn if it stopped for longer than one second in the same spot. Meanwhile, a hawk circles the same shady cacti but with a different intention in mind, other than cooling itself.

The silence is a separate entity living up here in its completeness, in the middle of hundreds of square miles, deprived of the sounds of civilization.

Back in the car, we turn on the air conditioning to the highest setting and breathe in the cool air as if our lives depended on it. We continue breathing in and out, loudly and relieved while the winding road, wavy as a yellow ribbon, brings us reinvigorated but hungry into Junction, Texas, at mile 1,473. We drive up and down the main street of this town with a population of 2,000 people, in search of a barbecue restaurant, but all we can find effortlessly are shops that sell cowboy boots, spurs, and belt buckles.

Google Maps finally takes us to Lum's Bar-B-Que Restaurant, where I feast on my first brisket with a side of jalapeno coleslaw and pinto beans. This remains my favorite BBQ dish from all the American Southwest. For dessert, I get a jar of the house recipe pickled asparagus.

Satiated and still hot despite the cold beers we have for dinner, we decide that only the refreshing flowing waters of a river can bring our bodies back to a regular temperature. Ten more miles and we find ourselves in South Llano River State Park, where we get to enjoy the whole place by ourselves, as we are the only ones left there so late in the evening.

Floating carelessly between the rich vegetation-covered riverbanks, we make eye contact with turtles, which stick out their heads from the water from time to time, and with fireflies, their shapes perfectly outlined in the sunset light. We linger for a while, drying out in the sun now that it has lost some of its strong burning. Then, we drive back to the city, leaving behind goat farms and wild turkeys looking for food in the cactus bushes on the side of the road.

After such a long full day, we fell asleep like logs in a smoker's room No. 132, the only one available at the Rodeway Inn in Junction, TX.

# 4 - *CAVERNS OF SONORA, TX* ☼ *WHITE SANDS NATIONAL MONUMENT, LAS CRUCES, NM*

W e have not yet adjusted to the time zone. So, by 5 am, we have already had enough sleep. Even if we had not, we would still have to wake up and be ready to go by six. The desert sun is even more diligent than we are, and by 9 am is already burning full throttle. Therefore, every morning we try unsuccessfully to beat it. After refusing a breakfast of pancakes, waffles, muffins, and donuts, we leave Junction at mile 1,494, heading to the Caverns of Sonora.

When M. planned every destination of our trip, he carefully picked a cave for diversity. Among all the exotic landforms we will explore, he snuck in a morning underground stroll.

Being so matutinal, as I was saying, we arrive an hour early for the first guided group tour of the cave. This gives us enough time to sightsee. It is a private area meant to keep its visitors busy all day long. You can even spend the night here if you have a recreational vehicle to park or a tent to set up. There are trails for hiking, picnic areas, a visitor center, a restaurant, and a souvenir shop. The predecessors of the family owning this place discovered the cave in 1955 and turned it into a tourist attraction. It has served as such ever since 1960.

This ranch is situated literally in the middle of the desert, but because it is inhabited, the entire area is a green oasis that attracts deer, peacocks, and squirrels that have made the Caverns of Sonora their home. We also see swallows in nests feeding their chicks and a bat flying chaotically between the branches of a tree. I get to see my first teepee here, the canvas tent that the Native Americans used to live in, and I have to say it is a lot roomier than it appears.

I have visited quite a few caverns in my life and all of them impressed me with the infinite patience they must have to grow their stalactites and stalagmites. For millions of years, time seems to have stood still, although you can hear it dripping from the ceiling, creating astounding geological formations that scientists can study for generations on end. I have to admit that I prefer the above landscape, pulsing with life and furry animals, to this underground natural palace. Nevertheless, I would never say no to a speleology lesson.

What makes this cavern different are the bacon stalagmites, resembling my favorite American breakfast, and straw stalactites that are long, thin and tubular. But what specifically makes the Sonoran cavern special is the butterfly stalactite, a geological formation resembling the delicate insect. The interesting fact about it is that it was vandalized back in 2006, and the culprit broke and stole the right wing of the butterfly. I wonder what it is that triggers a person to destroy the beauty of nature. What does that say about us humans? In this situation, not even the $20,000 ransom for reuniting the stalagmite with its limb was motivating enough for the culprit to straighten the wrongful deed. Could this have something to do with a competing cavern?

We leave in search of lunch at mile 1,563, but we arrive in a dwelling of some sort only after 250 miles. As I said, everything is immense here in the US, including distances between inhabited places. With just a few intersecting roads and a population of 1,760, the town proudly wears the serious name of Van Horn. For hours, we see nothing notable, just the desert, the sturdy highway, and a four-engine train dragging at least a hundred wagons filled with merchandise from China.

We parted with Van Horn at mile 1,819, after having eaten a delicious Mexican lunch at Lizzy's Torteleria. It is an authentic Mexican restaurant in every way: traditional food served with rice, beans, homemade tortilla, and jalapenos. The interior design comprises yellow-orange and green painted walls, corrugated paper cacti and sombrero decorations hanging from the ceiling, crucifixes, ponchos, and plastic flowers strewn about. The soundtrack on the radio seems to be broadcast from somewhere across the border. English has a strong Spanish accent in these parts of the country.

The same scenery runs for 200 more miles in the other direction, as we drive on what appears to be an endless highway. The horizon outlines the Guadalupe Mountains interrupted here and there by the thorns of some old cacti or a grandiose ranch gate. As we are the only ones in this vast land, we put the car in park several times to take pictures of the magnificent open road, with the two yellow lines as our central element, dividing for miles and miles the desert beauty.

The ranch gates and a few stray cows grazing close to the side of the road, over the almost invisible wire fence, are the only proof of life in the area. We keep asking ourselves how they can survive in this climate and on a diet of dry bushes, weeds, and thistles. But, we cannot come up with an answer.

The rest of the day is more dream than reality, because what I get to see and feel is hardly believable. The heat is over 100°F and tumbleweeds are rolling down the asphalt. We pass by some salt dunes right after crossing the border to New Mexico. Here, I go through my first border patrol checkpoint, in Alamogordo to be more exact, and then we arrive at the White Sands National Monument. The Desert Haven.

We enter the park late in the afternoon when the sun has lost its power to fade colors. The scenery changes a few shades, going from light beige and grey to pure white, speckled by the green of the cacti and shrubs. Gradually, the vegetation disappears entirely the deeper we drive into the park until all that is left for the eye to see is a vast area of white dunes. The contrasting blue of the sky intensifies strongly to the West.

Scientifically, this is the largest area in the world covered with an abundance of gypsum and selenite crystals. As if in a fairy-tale, a sea of magic dust surrounds us. A 270-square mile immaculate sea.

For several hours, I am acting as a little girl would. I make snow angels in the sand. I roll down the hill, and bury my legs in the sand pretending to be a mermaid with a sparkling white tail. I draw smiley faces and hearts with M.'s and my initials inside and fight with sand balls. M. has his own adorable little boy moment that is not about rolling through the sand but sitting down and talking to it as if it were his friend:

*"How have you been, old friend? It has been so long since we've seen each other..."*

We walk up and down the wavy white dunes, leaving behind silly traces that the wind will wipe off as if we were never here. Us and a million other people that have enjoyed this wonder so far, including the cast of the first Transformers movie. There are so many dunes that we are sovereigns over a few of them at a time. Then, we end up on dunes mastered by other families who have probably spent their entire day here. Kids slide down the hill in sleds or floats, and their laughter resounds across the valley.

Just like in all the other parks, the place is flawlessly orchestrated to welcome the visitors without damaging nature. Here and there parking lots and roofed picnic areas offer shelter in the total lack of shade. There are grills, trashcans, and ecological toilets.

A few passionate drivers take advantage of the flat and vast surface between the dunes and start a game of drifting, intentionally oversteering with the rear slipping and drawing a full circle in the sand. It does not take long before the ranger drives up to them with the siren on and politely asks them to stop and leave the drifting to Vin Diesel in *The Fast and The Furious*.

The sun is close to setting for the day, stretching our shadows onto the sand, which gives us reason to take photos of our long reflections jumping, kissing, and holding hands. As the horizon dramatically reddens, we have the most romantic dinner on the sand, with pickled asparagus from Lum's Bar-B-Que and leftovers from Lizzy's Tortilleria.

We barely say goodbye to the now cold and refreshing sand, as the night falls and the only distinguishable things are the taillights of the cars. While we exit the park, we notice that they have already cleared the sand from the road, probably with a snowplow that leaves behind sand piles on the shoulders. It makes sense why they do it, as everything that is cleared out at dusk, the wind will completely undo by dawn. The footsteps are now slowly vanishing from the dunes and car traces from the road, and the scene becomes anew again. We feel as if we are gliding among snowy hills.

After such a rich experience, one would expect us not to care about anything anymore, and just keep our thoughts faithful to the White Paradise, dreaming of those children sliding in sleds in the middle of the summer. Unfortunately, twenty miles before Las Cruces, our last stop for the day, the red flames of wildfire appear on the dark background of the sky. The more we approach it, the brighter it gets. It now looks like a major forest fire; the traffic slows down and then it stops. Fire trucks block the road and police officers explain the situation to every driver and ask them to turn around. The sight is frightening and stands in contrast with the pristine place from which we are coming. A few days later, we would find out that they could not contain the fire that night, and it continued to spread.

Throughout our trip, we encountered several wildfires and heard about some more on the news, not just in these desert parts but in the mountains of California and Montana too. All the way from Texas to California, the authorities take extreme measures to prevent these fires. In some places, they even forbid outside smoking.

Stopped by the police on our way to Las Cruces, we took a detour on Route 70 and drove 130 miles (instead of only twenty) to reach the same Best Western hotel in Las Cruces. This 110-mile deviation takes us a second time through the Border Patrol in Alamogordo. We are both tired, and M. has to drive two more hours. I keep dozing off and waking up terrified that lizards and foxes are crossing the road in front of us, and then I try to warn M. not to run them over. After 776 miles farther and another day intensely lived, we fell asleep in room 201, dreaming of snow angels in white sand and bright red flames on the hills of New Mexico.

# CHAPTER IV -
## *ARIZONA, THE GRAND CANYON STATE*

# 5 - *TOMBSTONE, TUCSON, PICACHO PEAK, PHOENIX, RIMROCK, AZ*

A t mile 2,260, we leave Las Cruces, New Mexico, and enter Interstate 10, which takes us to Arizona, The Grand Canyon State. I open a double espresso coffee can that tastes like a liquid dessert. Soon enough, I discover that one thing this trip lacks is good coffee. The hotels serve it for breakfast, but the dark-colored water does not taste like coffee. It just carries its name; therefore, I avoid it. I try to broaden my horizon and buy different canned or bottled coffee from the supermarket, but they are all really just "diabetes in a cup". Still, I have to satisfy my addictions. So, I test all the brands available at gas stations and 7Eleven stores and do my best to squeeze out the necessary caffeine every morning. As we hardly ever drive through any city, where I could probably find decent coffee shops, I have to be thankful for what I have.

While my taste buds separate the coffee from the sugar in a contemplative manner, all I see out of the car window is desert, interrupted occasionally by trains hauling hundreds of wagons. It looks like it is going to be a nice touristic and relaxing day, and the temperature will only rise to pancake-baking levels. It is one of those days when we dress casually, in sneakers and wrinkled t-shirts.

Soon, we reach Tombstone, the first and probably only historic place on our list. I admit, if I were a man, my enthusiasm would go a few levels higher. Even so, I appreciate a five-star cinematic morning.

All the Western movies I have watched in my life seem to have been filmed here, on this particular Main Street. Cowboys with spur boots, sheriffs with frock coats and shiny badges on the lapel, guns carried ostentatiously, wide-brim hats, leather pants, ladies wearing ribbon bonnets in light color tones matching their tight corset dresses, carriages, saloons, shady ladies, trading posts, and horses. All of them are perfectly preserved from the turn of two centuries ago. I don't remember the frequency, but in the evenings, there are stage performances of the famous confrontations between the villains and the sheriff where Kevin Costner, Val Kilmer, and Kurt Russell always end up victorious on screen, blowing gunpowder out of the gun barrel and then sticking the gun back in its sheath.

Then there are the souvenir shops with Wyatt Earp, OK Corral, Doc Holliday, or just Wild-Wild-West merchandise. Felt hats, big buckle belts, rattle snake-shaped mugs, decorative horseshoes, and toy guns. I forgot to ask about a good cup of coffee though, among all of these memorabilia. In the same stores, but on different shelves, or different stores altogether, there is Native American merchandise, mostly Navajo and Zuni. I find the way these two inhomogeneous worlds blend here very interesting. Even for commercial purposes, having them displayed next to each other seems inadequate. Jewelry, sculptures, toys, quilts, statues, carpets, bags, dream catchers, and old tribe maps invite you to consider them closely. Maybe this is out of the collective guilt of white people, or maybe just because everything is handmade and not mass-produced in China.

We leave Tombstone at mile 2,498 going North-West on Interstate 10. The same polychrome desert is everywhere I look, but the closer we get to Tucson, taller and taller candle-like cacti pierce the horizon. M. told me about them, about the Saguaro cacti and their encounter years ago. He recalled how he stepped out of the car to look at them closer and exchange a few kind words. I know M. well, and this seems like a typical approach:

*"How are you, my friend?"*

The cactus replies, of course. It tells M. about the people passing by and about how it sees them from high up there, without intervening.

Truth is that you can spot them from the side of the road and all you want is to get a closer look, to touch them, and maybe understand a little better how a living thing can stand so straight and unflinching, without being overwhelmed by the torrid sun they breathe under.

We pull over every time we see a cactus close to the road and walk up to it. We try to touch it with our index finger, avoiding the millions of protective thorns and try to take in the whole thing from bottom to top, shielding our eyes from the sun with our hands. Photographing its entire stalk challenges our artistic abilities. Going around it to find the perfect photo angle is like stepping on a minefield but with short cacti, thistles, and other prickly desert plants. We do not give up though without stealing away their fantastic apparition and saving it into our pictures.

We get even more excited when we see taller ones, or short and chubby ones, or with more arms, or with red succulent flowers, or with the lower part nibbled by wildlife. Once we are up in Sentinel Peak, where the Tucson panorama is widely visible, we find ourselves in a cacti forest. It appears that the desert can be wooded. By cacti. As much as we can hold out against the Arizonian midday sun, each of us holding a bottle of water like it was gold, we walk among them, point at every funny looking shape we encounter, and fill the camera's memory with these otherworld creatures.

Back at the car, we feel we should learn more about the Saguaros, and what we find out online is nothing but extraordinary. The thorns are their leaves that become thin, rigid, and pointy so that they won't eliminate water through them. When they reach around thirty-five years of age they start growing flowers and only the ones that get to live to be a hundred years old or more start growing arms. Meaning branches. Inside their trunks, they stock all the water they can after every desert rain. If you touch them, you notice they are boiling.

Birds prick the cacti and drink their water, and so do other animals by biting into their lower parts where the thorns are scarce or dried. Despite these predators, they stand tall and survive with dignity.

We have lunch close by, at Catalina BBQ Golf Club, where we are the only customers at this hot hour. There is a gorgeous terrace facing the green golf course where we would rather eat, but being out there feels like breathing inside a tiny room with ten heaters turned on high. Therefore, we stay inside, under the cool breeze of the AC. We temporarily forget that outside these walls and windows breathing is rather a voluntary act of taking in hot air and praying you won't choke.

In this part of the country, you can't go wrong with whatever barbeque dish you choose. Pulled pork, turkey, chicken, brisket, or sausages. Hence, we always order a sampler to try them all. Many restaurants brag about their barbeque sauce and their special recipe for preparing and smoking the meat. Here, they have sour, sweet and spicy sauces, and their brisket is to die for.

We continue driving on the same Interstate 10, which connects Jacksonville, Florida to Los Angeles, California, traveling from East to West for almost 2,500 miles. We get closer to Phoenix, Arizona, where we would arrive in less than two hours. However, we prefer to go around this five million people urban area and just admire it from afar.

We drive up to Picacho Peak, at about a 3,300-foot altitude, from where we can see the city skyline and its suburbs. The landscape is stunning in the sunset light, with the Sonoran Desert in the background, the volcanic rocks dotting the winding horizon, and the planes taking off or landing every five minutes at Sky Harbor Airport.

We walk around the park to find the perfect spot to savor the sight and decide to take shelter from the heat under the walls of a little old fort. I cool off with a Mike's Hard Lemonade concealed in an opaque water bottle, and then an unexpected show begins. A slender blonde young woman carrying a large camera and a handsome black young man take the scene. He seats himself artistically and slightly dangerously on a crag while she takes pictures of him, squinting and smiling. The atmosphere heats up when he takes off his shirt and completes the urban scene behind him with his athletic figure.

We spend the night at Beaver Creek Inn, in Rimrock, in the cutest and most comfortable room so far. I cannot remember its number, but it might have had a name instead, like Roadrunner, Desert Flower, Waterfall, or Red Robin.

# 6 - *SEDONA, DEVIL'S BRIDGE, CATHEDRAL ROCK, SLIDE ROCK STATE PARK, FLAGSTAFF, AZ*

E arly in the morning, I sip my coffee in complete silence and chill, in the shade of a plump pine tree, on the patio outside the room. The wrought-iron table and chair, from where I admire the yet sleepy little town, lies three steps from the tarmac. It is so delightful having a cup of Joe in my PJs, in the street. I almost have no hard feelings about the brand-new bra I have forgotten back in that room.

After a relaxing day of cruising around, we flex our muscles for a few ambitious hikes. We fill up the cooler with water bottles and ice, put on our hiking clothes and shoes that still have their original color.

Under the exquisitely blue sky, we navigate a region of the Coconino National Forest, somewhat concerned when the car thermometer already shows 100°F at only 9 am. At mile 2,835, we enter Sedona, where every other mile a giant electronic billboard warns the people of the extreme heat and forbids bonfires and outside grilling and smoking.

I forget about the heat and dangers when we arrive downtown, not because my memory resembles a rusted colander, which it does, but because I have never seen such a jewel of a city before in my life. M. tells me that this is a particularly expensive area, which quickly becomes clear It just looks like a custom-made town. Everything is spotless. The architecture is elegant, uniform, in complementary tones of yellow, purple, and teal.

For the last ten miles before turning up in Sedona, the landscape evanesced its hue to the brick-red Navajo stone. The city spreads out in the middle of an unearthly picturesque desert spot, carpeted with short pine timbers, ravines, and coral cliffs called buttes and mesas. Conceivably, they carry a commonsense name such as the Red Rock State Park. The entire downtown is color-coordinated and built out of the materials that spotlight the scenery. The LED signs of every store, hotel, restaurant, and even McDonald's match the same palette. Nothing stands out with extravagant fonts or excessive advertising. We drive by many art galleries and some of the most elaborate decorative windmills. To visit this ingenious urban creation and discover that people can preserve it is a delight.

This place energizes me with its visionary-optimistic look, and I can't wait to explore the Navajo sandstone landmass around it. I feel somehow familiar with these surroundings, because a short while before this trip, I had watched Book Club, a romcom, most of it filmed in Arizona. As I was telling you earlier, and I was not lying, my knowledge of America is mostly movie-related and has deep roots in cinematic productions. So, in the movie, Andy Garcia, who lives in Sedona, invites Diane Keaton over to his house for drinks. While the sunset deepens the color of the wild buttes in the distance, they enjoy a glass of wine on the terrace. He then takes her on a private plane ride above the Red Rocks, showing her around and flying nonchalantly over the Cathedral Rock. Although unaware at the time, I will soon visit the same spot myself, only not in flight.

This is how we end up as extras on a Hollywood movie set when we start the first hike of the day. We are heading to the Devil's Bridge on a sandy trail that later inclines abruptly and lays the initial coat of color to our hiking shoes. It is still early in the morning but the air is getting harder to breathe. Being a famous destination in Arizona, the trail is lively with visitors of all ages and nationalities. We encounter couples, families with children, groups of teenagers, and loners, all walking in the same direction as we are, or already returning to the parking lot. I notice them smiling and greeting us, and with some of them we even exchange a few words. I love it, and I get used to it in no time, as all the Americans we meet along the way are just as cordial.

You get to meet fellow hikers on the trails, and if they are American, they address you or at least smile at you. Eye contact does not seem to be a difficult act for them but rather usual. The small talk can be brief:

"Hi, how are you?"

"Great, thanks. How are you?"

"Alright / Great / Good."

Alternatively, they can be more elaborate. Like when you reach the top and admire the view, or take photos, or simply catch your breath just like everybody else around:

"Where are you from?"

"I am from Europe, Romania."

"Wow, I've heard it's a beautiful country. And what's your name?"

"Raluca."

"Such an interesting name. Met no one with that name before."

The conversation can go on about different topics, like weather or itinerary:

"Where are you going next? / Where have you already been? / Isn't this a wonderful day? / Can't believe how hot it is! / Isn't this amazing? / It was worth the hike, wasn't it?"

Or to pay you a compliment:

"Funny T-shirt. / Love your hair! / Wow, you have a great tan! / You made it to the top. Congratulations!"

It is so easy to slip compliments into the chat or just to be nice and bring a smile to somebody's face. It might be because people pay attention to their peers and nothing stops them from expressing their admiration. There are no barriers to communication in nature, and I wonder if this also occurs in the streets or on their way to work.

I witness the same pattern while waiting in line at the gas station restroom or the cash register. Almost every time I end up conversing with my neighbor. Their attitude is contagious, and I now have the tendency to look for something remarkable in everyone I meet so that I can pay them a compliment. But this only works here, in the States. I tried doing this back at home in Romania, but the people got confused, and I felt like a freak with no excuse for my behavior. Conversation arises naturally here, because the locals are used to it, and they always have a witty reply up their sleeve. In Romania, it feels like my compliment hits a wall and is not able to get the other person out of their thoughts.

If I am climbing and they are descending and notice my red face and heavy breathing, they say something encouraging, knowing that it had been hard for them to climb too:

*"Great job, you're almost there! / Doing good, the hardest part is almost over. / Keep going. It's worth it!"*

Their kindness comes in handy when there is just M. and me, and we would like to have a photo with the incredible landscape behind us, but a selfie would not suffice. This is when they step in to help and turn from strangers into friends. Smiling, they offer to take the photo and say something like:

*"What a nice couple! / Here you go, it is a great shot!"*

*"Oh, thank you so much!"*

*"You're welcome! Enjoy the rest of the day."*

The same phenomenon happens here. Once we arrived on the Devil's Bridge, a giant cliff that time and weather carved inexplicably into an archway to another world, we found ourselves in need of a kind American tourist. There is one! We approach a woman we believe to be an expert in photography because of the large camera she carries around her neck. She offers to take a picture of us in the center of the scene, with the bridge beneath us. In the picture, she skillfully squeezes the entire desert beneath us, with its shrub forests and oddly shaped red rocks to which only the Native Americans alone could give a proper name.

We head back down, overwhelmed by the National-Geographic-worthy featured location, still in decent shape and with plenty of energy left. The backpack is now lighter due to all the water we consumed up on the bridge and the skin on our arms and foreheads is a darker shade of tan.

M. informs me that next on our list is Cathedral Rock, and I become childishly impatient to see myself up on top of a crag with such a resounding name and full of pride for being able to ascend it. Even more so, since this is the rock Andy Garcia shows Diane Keaton from his private jet.

The age on my ID shows I'm somewhere halfway along my lifespan, assuming I'm lucky enough to live to be eighty years old. Thus, any victory I get over altitude or extreme climate conditions fills my heart with satisfied sighs and builds up my self-esteem like nothing else could.

We are on our way to the trailhead with the AC on high, to refresh ourselves as much as possible before stepping outside into the sauna. After parking, we fill up the backpack with extra water bottles, spray every visible inch of skin with SPF 70 sunscreen, and put ice-cold wet buffs on our heads. It is almost lunchtime, and the thermometers will read the highest temperatures of the day right when we are halfway up the trail. Still, we must go through with our plan, because if we don't, Cathedral Rock would remain unconquered, as tomorrow the trip takes us some place further.

We own the hot situation we are dealing with and head to the trail. We are determined to hike the one-mile distance and a 525-foot elevation like pros who have just climbed four and a half miles up to the Devil's Bridge. Hm. As long as the road winds on a flat surface or at a slightly inclined angle, my effort will sustain. The belief that the sun is pressing on my head while struggling to keep me in place surely stands out from all the other random thoughts that cross my mind. The bliss of being in Arizona, the gratitude for my former swimmer's body that still works, and the astonishment of being able to carry it up on the Cathedral Rock, are losing ground at the moment.

As soon as the angle extends, we switch from walking to a steep climb and must develop an ascending strategy. Using our hands, we climb giant boulders that resemble rising dough balls growing on top of each other. The exertion of lifting my body higher and higher, while the heat causes the rocks to burn and the skin to redden, raises my pulse at an alarming pace that makes it difficult for me to breathe. From now on, after every ten steps of arduous escalating, I have to stop and catch my breath in the shade of any dwarf or balding tree that I encounter on the crimson crags.

I fight the heat that makes my blood boil. My leg muscles feel like rocks lifting hundreds of pounds of flesh, and the voice in my head keeps telling me to give up, that this rock is not worth putting myself in danger. Despite everything, I persist, eager to reach the summit and have this exotic world at my feet. I am lucky that M.'s voice is more persuasive than the internal one imploring me to end my exhaustion. I am so lucky he encourages me on every rough trail of this fantastic trip.

M. is the sort of mountain creature who becomes more agile as the slope steepens. A hard path for me seems to him as easy as an escalator that propels him higher and faster than my eyes can even follow. He is so comfortable up here, just like a fish in the water, or more like a mountain goat up on the sloped scree of Mount Whitney. Being here means pure happiness, and it does not matter to him if we climb ten feet per minute. He is patient and trusting that I won't surrender. I will do my best not to miss any summit, especially THE supreme trek at the end of our trip when we will climb Mount White, over 14,000 feet high.

He trusts the magic of these places, which I too feel in my chest as soon as I find myself up there, looking over this newly discovered planet. From this height, the landscapes resembles nothing of what I am used to from back home. The landmarks seem to have been subdued to foreign laws of nature, which gave birth to this decor. One would expect to find them populated by unearthly creatures and not human beings. It seems even more unreal to find myself here, my heart exploding with satisfaction.

All the pictures we take up here standing in the center of this endless red rock world, next to many purple ear-shaped blooming cacti, look more photo-shopped than loyal reflections of reality.

The extreme altitude and the spectacular rocky crags allow us to take photos with a high degree of difficulty. Exchanging cameras with a newlywed couple who came here for their honeymoon, we immortalize each other somehow suspended above the terrain. We are Kate and Leo at the top of the bow, flying over the ocean-like desert. We rest in the shade of a cylindrical rock as high as a ten-story building and lay down, hoping to absorb as much coolness as possible to last us until we get back in the car.

Downhill is unquestionably easier, but just until we get to the over-risen doughy boulders. We have to lean on our hands to dismount them. Meanwhile, the temperature has gone up to 113°F, and the sizzling rocks burn my palms. I splash drinking water on my hands, lean on them and try to climb down as quickly as possible to avoid singeing my skin. At one point, M. puts down the water bottle to free his hand and help me jump off a paunchy stone. When he picks it up again, we notice that the bottom of the bottle has melted and starts dripping. My survival instinct kicks in at the sight of the pierced plastic, and I start running down back to the parking lot.

Hiking back, I spot things I have missed on the way up. There are billboards at the trailhead with information about the geology and history of this place, about the people that discovered it and transformed it into a natural preserve for others to explore. A few other signs educate tourists about flora, fauna, and how to stay safe among wild animals.

The message is always the same: we are visitors in the house of wild animals. We are encouraged to let the animals be and not to feed them, as this is their habitat and they can take care of themselves without human help. The other advice we have found written on small boards throughout the park is, *"Do not burst the crust."* Indeed, the dirt is extremely interesting here, looking like a crunchy caramel layer with a variety of plants and delicate lizards swarming from underneath. Every step taken outside the trail risks destroying something nature created with such care.

The day is still young and so much has already happened under the intense Arizonian sun. We are eager to add to our afternoon agenda any other nearby destination, as long as it involves shade and water. I can imagine in vivid detail the sounds my skin will make the moment it meets water. I imagine a sizzling frying pan that, when put under the running water, is bubbling noisily and spattering all over.

We drive north on shadowy routes through the Coconino National Forest and enter the Slide Rock State Park. This is another noteworthy place on my I-haven't-seen-something-like-this-in-my-life list. Ten miles north of Sedona, the Oak Creek flows through the canyon of the same name, and a slippery river bed forms between its tall red walls. The entire area turns into an aquatic park where children and adults dive into the river waters and glide down on a natural slide that goes for roughly a mile.

We put on our swimming suits and the water shoes we bought precisely for this type of occasion and apply a generous layer of sunscreen. With the backpack refilled with water bottles and snacks, we set out upriver into the canyon in search of a spot in the shade where we can also soak in the cool waters. As soon as we pass the areas where the creek runs over the rocky plaits of the canyon, carrying downhill shrieking kids and adults, we get to a portion of the park that is wide and peaceful. Having left our stuff on the shore, we dip up to our chins in the cool mountain water, waiting for our bodies to return to a reasonable temperature, sizzling and bubbling, just as I imagined.

For a few hours, we are spoiled and refreshed. I read Wild, and M. naps on the bank. Then, we befriend a couple from Nashville, Tennessee, who are vacationing with their kids. Before they leave, they ask us to take a picture of them. So, I do my artistic best and create a family portrait that they will place on the mantel above the fireplace when they get back home.

Less than an hour north of Sedona is Flagstaff, where we arrive at mile 2,885. In such a short time, we find ourselves first in a desert resort and then in a ski resort, with pine forests and ski cable cars. We eat dinner at Fat Olive, and then call it a night in room 318, thinking of Humphrey's Peak that we will climb early in the morning when the sun has not yet shown its fangs.

# 7 - *NAVAJO NATION, TUBA CITY, GLEN CANYON, LAKE POWELL, PAGE, HORSESHOE BEND, HOLBROOK, AZ*

T he next day, fully equipped for the mountain trail and physically and mentally prepared to climb it, we were forced to turn around due to the extreme heat. Being an unusually hot summer that has already caused wildfires out West, the authorities closed most of the trails to prevent other disasters from happening.

During the six weeks of our North-American vacation, we get to meet and talk with so many people, and the stories they tell with such ease seem like movie scripts to me. It might be the fact that land, oceans, and perhaps fifty years of evolution separate my country from this one. It could also be because the stories told in another language tend to be far more interesting. Nevertheless, no matter what makes them so special, we are usually open to listening to the people we meet. Curiosity increases my interaction with fellow travelers since I noticed how sociable they are.

The same thing happens with a Greek-American man with whom we happen to share a table at breakfast this morning at the Baymont Inn and Suites in Flagstaff. There was a large group of Asian guests in the hotel restaurant, swarming like a beehive, bumping into us in their pursuit for the last piece of omelet. It was so crowded that we could not find a single place to sit and eat. We revolve around our axis, plates in hand, thinking we'd better hit the road instead, when surprisingly this man, terribly amused with the chaos, invites us to sit at his table.

We shortly find out that he was born in Greece and moved here when he was eighteen years old to study engineering at Northern Arizona University in Flagstaff. He has been a teacher for many decades at a university in California and cannot get used to old age. Back in Greece, he has a brother who hardly gets by because of the economic crisis, and he has to send him money to help. He finds California ridiculously expensive, and he barely survives on a teacher's salary. This week, he had returned to the city for his fortieth college reunion. He recalls how Flagstaff used to be during his student years when wild woods went on for miles. Whenever his parents had come to visit, they could hardly find accommodations. There were no hotels here back then. Now there are tens of them filled by millions of tourists who visit the Grand Canyon in the summer and the ski slopes in the winter. He misses the city as it used to be, all green and quiet, and resents it, as it is now, crammed with buses and invading tourists. I understand him, even if I am one of those invading tourists.

We successfully check out and uproot the luggage from the reception hell, where apparently hundreds of people try to do the same. We then have to reconfigure the itinerary without conquering Humphrey's Peak because of the hellacious weather. So, we head north to Page, Arizona.

Native Americans populate over 23,000 square miles of desert in North-East Arizona. Navajo, Zuni, and Hopi tribes call this barren land their home. The landscape looks selenic and uninhabitable with hills and Navajo sandstone rocks and formations of all heights and shapes. The capital of the territory is Tuba City, where we arrive at mile 2,985.

Downtown we find a museum and a trading post where I can hardly decide what dreamcatcher and earrings to buy for myself as souvenirs. Most of the traditional merchandise is handmade of silver, feathers, bone, wool, and semi-precious stones. They make me think of ancient times with their rudimentary and charming patterns. They are so colorful and alive, shaped like mythical animals and birds. Every item tells an old story about the secret to happiness and wisdom in a language only the Native Americans speak. Touching the jewelry and decorations, I believe I might learn something about their spirits. I am again as happy as a little girl with my new turtle coral earrings, and I feel as if I am wearing a piece of the universe's magic.

We pass 3,000 miles when we enter the Glen Canyon Recreational Area, where we spend most of the day. This is the place where the Colorado River twirls its silky green waters like a contortionist dragon. Over a length of almost 200 miles, the stream separates Arizona from Utah, and the walls of the canyon hold it captive, forming the largest reservoirs in the United States. Two million tourists visit Lake Powell every year, including us this summer.

When I end up in the desert looking at so much water, all I can think about is diving noisily in its midst. This is exactly what we do as soon as we discover where Wahweap Swimming Spot is, a maintained area with all the necessary facilities. From the parking lot to the beach, we walk covered in towels head to toe, not trusting that the sunscreen can handle temperatures that are high enough to roast chestnuts. Also, we have to wear the water shoes as the soles of our feet would one hundred percent become crispy as bacon by the time we'd get to the loch.

We leave our stuff on the lakeside and dart to the water, which is refreshing enough so that we barely notice that it is somewhat warm, but we don't mind. We wallow with satisfied faces, defying the heat that is still reigning over the land.

At some distance from the beach, a boat ramp gets our attention. One by one, cars driving backward launch motorboats into the lake. I imagine how fun it must be for boat and yacht owners to spend weekends and vacations floating in this tricolor landscape of water, sky, and red rock. I would not say no to a few lazy days onboard, reading in the shade, but this is not the purpose of our trip.

Therefore, we continue exploring on the other side of the lake, at Chains Swimming Area, in Utah. This is a wild rocky spot, which younger people prefer for extreme sports, like diving from its steep banks into the deep water. The only extreme thing about what we are doing is climbing down the canyon walls that feel as hot as a ceramic pot forgotten in the oven overnight. The soles of our shoes don't have enough time to melt from the parking lot to the lake, and this makes me think they were worth the price.

We maintain our body temperatures with a delicious Hawaiian Big Wave Golden Ale and enjoy the landscape. This place looks foody, like giant pastries layered with vanilla and caramel filling and dunked in waves of absinthe.

All the swimming in the sweet desert made us hungry. So, we stopped for an early dinner in Page, Arizona at Big John's Texas BBQ. In these places, as I said before, you cannot go wrong with barbeque. There are metal buckets filled with raw peanuts in shell placed on every table so that you can nibble on something until you get your order. We decide on a sampler with a bit of all the smoked meats they serve, accompanied by potato salad, chili, a garden salad with croutons, and corn on the cob with butter. We eat all of it as the day has worn us out, and recharge our batteries.

The restaurant is packed, and there are tourists at every table, alone or with families and friends. They talk among themselves or with their neighbors as if they all know each other. There is an old man next to our table whose demeanor is fascinating to me; he eats by himself but is constantly talking to us and to a group of people from another table. It is such an incredible thing not to feel lonely among people, even when you are traveling by yourself.

There are 200 more miles to go until the bed will hug our tanned, traveled, and tired bodies, and give them back to us tomorrow completely rested. Until then, we stopped to visit Horseshoe Bend, just outside Page.

The Colorado River, which has never in its entire existence, left anything boring behind - winds around a huge cliff, forming this unlikely shape of a horseshoe before continuing its course. Three million tourists visit this place every year. We walk a mile down to the canyon rim and another mile back on the hot sand, feeling sorry for the unfortunate ones that are wearing sandals or flip-flops.

In the dusk light, the landscape looks like a painting. Hundreds or maybe thousands of people are standing on the abrupt rim, over 300 feet high. They are watching the river run its waters on the white bank resembling thick green moss and carry yachts that look like tiny paper boats from up here. The canyon changes colors and becomes more orange and redder as the sun is heading to the precipice of the horizon. The green shades of the river turn blue and then purple, just like the peacock's feathers.

At mile 3,293, we arrive in Holbrook, Arizona. We park in front of the Days Inn Hotel, throw ourselves on the comfortable bed in room 215, and let the images of lakes, rivers, and canyons march through our random dreams.

# **8 -** *THE PETRIFIED FOREST NATIONAL PARK, CANYON DE CHELLY, AZ ☼ FARMINGTON, NM*

RALUCA BARBU

W e keep on exploring Arizona and spend the first half of the day in a former tropical forest turned to stone over a few hundred million years. It resembles a fragment from that fairytale about Aurora and Prince Philip, when Maleficent turns the kings and the courtiers to stone, but what happened here is even more intriguing. Climate and time had been plotting against nature for so long that they transformed the tree trunks from living organisms to semiprecious stones. I notice that all forests in the Sonoran Desert are some of nature's superlatives, and visiting them keeps me in a permanent state of awe.

There is nothing average about these places. The first settlers had exploited and devoured most of them, as they only saw a free source of raw material here, not a treasure of nature. Looking back over the history of humankind, this seems like a regular impulse, but only until the right people came along, discovered the value and uniqueness of these lands, and fought for their preservation for posterity. Changing the destiny of such gems spanned several decades, since their discovery before the 1900s, until they became a natural reserve protected by law.

The Petrified Forest National Park stretches out over a hundred square miles inside the Navajo and Apache lands, and the public has access to the most spectacular areas. The map we received when entering the park points to all the overlooks where you can drive up, park, and admire the badlands. I do not understand why this scenery would be referred to as bad when in reality there are endless hills of clay rocks with colorful names and unearthly looks.

Newspaper Rock, Rainbow Forest, Painted Desert, and Blue Mesa are a paradise to geologists and archeologists. They feast on all the petroglyphs and ruins left behind by the Pueblo people, the prehistoric fossils discovered in the Chinle area and the skeletons and petrified trunk sections exhibited in the museum.

For me, this is a journey in time into a graphic world, like a painting in a gallery where people not so different from me knew how to live a simple life, worshipping nature and stars, eating only what the earth would grow, and communicating their knowledge and art through drawings left on the badland rocks. At the same time, I walk into a future that has not yet destroyed the past. Instead, it keeps it secure in an hourglass for the hundreds of thousands of visitors who choose this destination every year.

We stop at every overlook and capture with our eyes and camera lenses the ocean of brick red built in uniformly chromatic layers of grey, white, light purple, beige, and brown, disturbed here and there by high or low waves. The terrain is made of a honey cake with walnut and vanilla filling, bitten and chewed on by the wind, with the entire selenic composition exposed to the elements.

We descend into the painting and drive through the Blue Mesa on a sinusoidal trail that carries us into a world kept captive in a magic globe. The acoustics are fantastic. The whispers are as loud as breathing and heartbeats. Just like in all the other parks, the trails are intended for hiking, to offer tourists a complex and teachable experience, while keeping them off the crust. Although the information panels mark every landmark we pass, I realize, as clear as the sky, that we are in the middle of a parallel universe.

At almost every vista, we meet the same tourists, because they are as overzealous as we are and do not want to miss anything on the map. We will see some of them later in the day at Canyon de Chelly, but the ones who make an impression on me are a New York couple traveling in a glittery black car.

Until we get back to the afternoon activities, we take a quick stop in Ganado, Arizona, at the Hubbell Trading Post National Historic Site for one of my purely feminine wishes. The store is impressive being set in the middle of the desert, away from the main road. Beyond the front door, the air I breathe seems to have been preserved from ancient times. The building is old and the wooden floors emanate a particular smell.

Before I can decide what jewelry would best suit me, I search every room. I bend down to look at all the merchandise and occasionally get the urge to touch it. There are plush dolls and animals, fabrics, wooden totems, old framed photographs, ceramic objects, masks made from leather and feathers, some scary, some friendly; stuffed horned animal heads, leather saddles, wool clothes and bags, jars with pickled cucumbers (that I have been seeing all around the Navajo Land); history books and long glass cases crammed with jewelry. It is so difficult to choose from the thousands of rings, bracelets, earrings, pendants, necklaces, and brooches. They are all made of silver combined with turquoise, opal, onyx, and coral. Each item is one of a kind, and all are excessively elaborate for my taste. I would have to change my entire wardrobe to match most of them. I decided on a Thunderbird bracelet, which is not an actual bird, but a mythical one, symbolizing life, truth, and energy, which used to be an emblem for many tribes.

At mile 3,469, we arrive in Chinle, Arizona, where we visit Canyon de Chelly, another niche touristic experience. In the center of the natural decor, lies a luxuriant green oasis, with cows and horses grazing unexpectedly green grass. The roads sinuate into the vast canyon, and a few pick-up trucks drive to modest houses.

We are in the Sonoran Desert, where the land is dry and bleached by the sun and the wind into pale shades. The vegetation is sparse and scattered but not inside the canyon. Between the 600-foot-tall walls, there are full-grown trees and pastures watered by the stream. Such a strong contrast of climate and geography, but the presence of humans is the most unexpected in this picture, though explicable. No wonder the Native Americans always found strategic places to settle and call home. About forty families still live here, despite all the cruel events that happened between the locals and the authorities over the years. This

National Monument preserves the original human presence.

We walk up to every overlook that offers a panoramic view of the incredible Navajo stone creations. We use superlatives every time we see an unusual rock sculpted as if by alien hands. I am afraid that I will soon have to recycle them, because my vocabulary is finite unlike the riches of this trip.

In most of the parking lots, there are Native Americans selling jewelry and trinkets out of the trunk of their cars, but they don't attract too many customers. I have already satisfied my desire to have something to remind me of these places. Even if I had not, it would not seem smart to shop for something of value on the side of the road.

Right at the end of the trail, there is the pièce de resistance, The Spider Rock. We forget time and space exist when we look at this masterpiece of nature and feel so happy that the Native Americans kept it to themselves, that it was not stolen from them like most of their land. The rock is 800 feet high and looks like a monolith with two uneven towers. It is 230 million years old and has profound significance in the mythology and folklore of the Hopi and Navajo tribes. It represents The Spider Woman or the Earth Goddess, the creator and protector of humans.

For this unlikely creation to exist, climate, time, and patience are once again to blame. Right at the crossing of two important canyons, De Chelly and Monument, this natural artifact stands erected, tall and narrow like the unfinished towers of Barcelona's famous cathedral, Sagrada Familia. It makes sense why the people of the past would give it supernatural powers. It is also clear why they filmed *Contact, The Lone Ranger,* and *Wild Wild West* here and many other cinematic productions.

The magic of this place moves us and pushes us to take many photos of the rock. Just when M. is about to take a picture of me with the view, an extremely nice and chatty old man approaches us and offers to take a photo of us both. He does just so, like a pro, despite his trembling hands. When he is about to leave, we thank him and he encourages us to walk further and see the Spider Rock. We don't know if he was joking and trying to make us believe we assiduously took photos of a nameless and meaningless rock, or whether his sight was not so good, or he just did not know which one the Spider Rock was altogether. Regardless of the truth, we amuse ourselves thinking that the old man missed the park's showstopper.

We enjoy a nice dinner right outside the reservation, at Junction Restaurant, a place with a traditional kitchen. As usual, we try something new and order aboriginal tacos and a Navajo Sheepherder sandwich made with Navajo bread, which resembles a fluffy yet crunchy Romanian fried donut. In addition, we have pickled cucumbers; I actually have seconds and thirds. The server is confused about why I keep asking for more pickles, but I don't care. The cucumbers are fantastic, and I recommend them!

At mile 3,673, we arrive in Farmington, New Mexico, where we spend the night at La Quinta Inn in room one hundred and something.

# 9 - *FOUR CORNERS, MONUMENT VALLEY NAVAJO TRIBAL PARK, DE MOTTE CAMPGROUND, AZ*

T his trip keeps on adding epithets to my travel journal and destinations with no echo of my previous experiences, despite my not so ignorant touristic agenda. We spend another day in Navajo Land, because historical and geographical monuments are plentiful in these parts.

First thing in the morning, at mile 3,735, we step into four states at once, the only place in the US where the corners of a quartet join. Four Corners Monument not only separates the semi-autonomous and self-governed territories of the Navajo and Ute tribes but also unites Utah, Colorado, Arizona, and New Mexico into a single point. *"Here we meet in freedom, under God, four states,"* decorates the metal plaque placed smack-dab in that point.

The existence of this spot has its origins at the end of the Civil War, when Congress wanted to create governments assigned to fight the spread of slavery and map out definitive borders between states. After several minor cadastral changes over several years, the four states fraternized and overlapped in this tip of the needle that has been serving for quite some time as a prop for the millions of tourists that have ever taken a photo here.

In most of the emblematical places M. planned for us to visit this summer, we had to wait in line to take photos of us together with the symbol in question. The same thing happens here. We wait patiently for couples and families to take their elaborate photos, smiling widely while having one limb in each corner so that they touch all four of them, or in less conventional postures like us, doing a pushup over the intersection with one palm or foot in each territory. If skeptics say you cannot be in two places at the same time, here you can be in four places and this makes it worth the wait.

The sun expands the obtuse angle with the East, raising the temperature of the asphalt and tainting the road with fata morgana as we head out to Monument Valley Navajo Tribal Park, one of the most spectacular and photographed places in the world. We are in the middle of the desert and at the same time at 5,575 feet of altitude. There are no mountains close by, as my preconceptions about altitude would make me believe.

The Marlboro commercials filming set lays before us.

For as far as you can see, with the naked eye or using binoculars, rocks resembling enormous pieces of 90% dark chocolate in the most unexpected shapes stand randomly scattered over a dark red decor, among dark green dusty shrubs.

The seventeen-mile sandy road meanders around the chocolaty sculptures, carrying hundreds of cars all around the park. We stop to watch almost every butte and mesa, terms that the natives who first discovered and inhabited these places invented but which do not have a Romanian translation. We try to identify the resemblance between the shapes and the names of the rocks: Elephant, Camel, Three Sisters, Thumb, Mittens, Dragon, Eye of the Sun, Bara Totem, and many others that only needed fifty million years to mirror something humanly familiar.

If I were to name them as I view this scenery for the first time, the cliffs appear to me as dinosaur fossils stubbornly standing in silly poses after millions of years. Monument Valley is, in fact, an outdoor museum where purple flower bushes grow directly in beautiful bouquets.

There are 145 square miles of the park, just as much blue sky above and dense heat between them, strong enough to roast large amounts of marshmallows. We park the car and follow the trails around the massive cliffs, some of them as tall as 1,000 feet and as voluminous as a cruise ship. We are two Lilliputians in a world sculpted by Gulliver. Or at least a couple of extras in a western.

This trip insists on strengthening my cinematic knowledge, taking me to movie sets. I am once more happy as a little girl, this time on Christmas morning! I have the same euphoric feeling right now, as I am trying to find the perfect words to describe my experience. The dominant sensation I have is that I have entered the TV set, and I am no longer sitting on the sofa watching a western, but I am acting in it. Any moment I am expecting cowboys to pass me by, riding on gorgeous stallions or in stagecoaches, leaving behind choking clouds of dust. Every time we are at the foot of a fortress-like rock, I try to spot Indians on top, armed with spears, bows, and arrows, defending it from the tourist invasion.

We change states once again, exiting Utah, *The Life Elevated State*, and return to Arizona, *The Grand Canyon State*. At a speed of at least fifty miles per hour, we advance towards the campground where an orange tent will be our home for the next two nights. We move down the map, but up to a higher altitude than the mountains in Romania. For a short while, we leave the desert and cross from East to West to the southern part of the Kaibab National Forest, while the roadside signs announce an altitude of 8,500 feet, higher than the tallest peak in the meridional Carpathians.

I am filled with both joy and sadness, a feeling I am getting used to from now on, as the scenery repeats itself every time we cross any forests from here to the Pacific. Two generations of timber share the same piece of land. A mature one utterly burned and a young one, fresh and dense, rising its green being from among the sharp scorched tips of its predecessor.

I have been learning so much about woodlands this month and a half. Not accidentally, the fire was the first and most unexpected lesson about their regeneration. Seemingly destructive, but in the long run a savior, fire is never-failing in the life of a forest.

Four hours later, at mile 4,081, we showed up at De Motte Campground, at nearly 9,000 feet above sea level and less than ten miles away from the Grand Canyon. We check into our camping site No. 12, as soon as the manager finds the reservation made by M. about three months ago. He then welcomes us and hands us the map. Yes, you always have to make reservations ahead for tent sites or cabins in the US national parks campgrounds, because by the end of spring and until late summer, all these places show a *"No vacancy"* sign at the entrance. This probably happens because of the big foreign tourist wave that annually invades the North American land, and because the locals are used to planning their vacations early in the year. M., as a local, was aware of the summer crowds and booked all the hotel rooms, cabins, and tent sites right after Santa Claus had left the building.

Having arrived here, I discover with amazement and delight what a campground can look like or rather should look like. Oh! Bear with me, please. I have waited so long to write about this topic!

There are RV, tent, or cabin campgrounds, separated or mixed. For example, De Motte only has RV and tent sites available. Since we do not have an RV, we unseal our brand-new orange tent and set it up in the designated area without an instruction manual. To the left, there is a parking place, to the right a picnic table with benches, a lamppost, and a fire pit. I find this fire pit both comfortable and romantic, but with this hot summer, even up here, at nearly 9,000 feet of altitude, bonfires and grilling are forbidden. Still, we get to enjoy them at the end of our trip, in Montana and Wyoming, where the heat is less intense as it is in the desert.

There are at least 150 feet between sites, enough to have privacy. Every five tents and two or three RVs or so, there is a restroom supplied with toilet paper and disinfectant dispensers. At this elevation, there is no indoor plumbing, but every restroom has a drinking water pump right next to the building. Now, do not imagine those plastic porta-potties installed by festival organizers. No, these are sturdy buildings, identical in all public and recreational areas all over America, and they all have composting toilets unless there is plumbing.

I insist on writing about toilets, because in Romania they just do not exist at higher altitudes. Or lower for that matter. Proof of that is all the areas surrounding the improvised mountain campgrounds where, for every patch of grass, you can find a used roll of toilet paper in different stages of decomposition.

Another great surprise for me is the wooden mini-amphitheater laid out near the entrance supplied with a screen, and enough benches to accommodate maybe twenty people. One could sit here and enjoy short movies or documentaries about the Arizonian flora and fauna or maybe photographs from past vacations, just like Helen Mirren and Donald Sutherland did in *The Leisure Seeker*. All one needs is a projector.

The humans orchestrated all of this, but what brings magic to this vacation spot is the wild background. Mature trees mingling with baby pines and birch trees comically sprouting from all directions; big or tiny fir cones fallen artistically on the ground; wildflowers; deer with large ears, birds with complicated Latin names. All coexist as if only for our amusement. Moreover, I am one very receptive girl to nature's harmony.

The sun is almost setting and on the trails between the improvised housings, young and old couples take their dogs around for a promenade, while a few groups of teenagers led by women with leadership skills loudly complete their evening summer camp activities. I would gladly take a walk myself, imprinting the whole place into my memory, and greet everyone with whom I cross paths. *"Hello. Have a wonderful evening!"* But I don't, because it is getting cold, and we have to prepare our dinner.

After a failed lunch at the only restaurant near Monument Valley, where I successfully ordered only deep-fried dishes, we scraped up a giant salad for dinner with all the ingredients from our cooler. Arugula from a box, cherry tomatoes from a bunch, peppers from a bag, tuna from a pouch, ranch dressing from a jar, and my new favorite cheese, Pepper Jack. We also have whole wheat bread that tastes like pound cake.

To me, sleeping in a tent is like an extreme sport I practice when the circumstances force me to. At the same time, it is also loaded with so many childhood memories, that I never say no to it. I can take the morning back pains and implicit fatigue, but what I have to fight the most is my mind. Separated from the wild by two thin layers of fabric, as impermeable and as strikingly colored as they may be, I imagine catastrophic scenarios with every swish and rustle that I hear. The same thing happens tonight. Far into the Wild West, in a dreamy campground, lighted by the moon and the stars, with M. peacefully snoring next to me unaware that I am fighting hungry beasts before falling asleep, I am exhausted by my imagination.

# 10 - *GRAND CANYON, AZ*

"**G**ood morning!" Says the manager, driving by our tent in a golf cart. "Where are you off to today?"

*"Good morning! We are going to see the Grand Canyon today!"*

*"Oh, great. It's a beautiful day for hiking! Have a good one."*

*"Thank you. You too!"*

After several ridiculous maneuvers, I imagine, that help me exit the tent keeping my balance and semi-professional camping dignity, I am finally bipedal without pulling a muscle or a hamstring. I do some easy knuckle cracking to regain my natural posture, as nonchalantly as possible. There will be no whining and complaining the day I get to visit the Grand Canyon! No way! The happiness of safely surviving the night and being awake overtakes the intensity of any fear for my physical integrity or back pains.

As soon as I taste the coffee from Meadow's Edge, a small *General Store* outside the campground, I forget about all the nocturnal and early day obstacles. This is my first strong and delicious coffee of the trip, and it amazes me to find it in a trailer turned into a café on the side of the road. I ordered an Americano with an extra shot of espresso, milk, and cinnamon. The taste of it makes me laugh at all the world's troubles and be more tolerant towards it. It was worth all of last night's restless sleep and will be worth the next one too. M. is not a coffee drinker, and he makes fun of my sudden exuberance and the fact that I can hardly hold the twenty-ounce cup that, according to the locals, is a regular size coffee!

We are very close to the Grand Canyon National Park North Rim entrance, just about ten miles away. However, we stop when we notice a wild buffalo herd grazing peacefully between the road and a pine forest. Later, we find out that this is one of the last seventeen herds left in the West.

We pull over behind another car and watch together with this couple, the wild buffalos going about their business as if there is no civilization around them, just endless forests and pastures inhabited by their peers. We take pictures and marvel at these Zen beings and the incredible luck we had to be in the right place at the right moment.

While all of this is going on, our neighbors brush their teeth with the skills of travelers used to brushing their teeth on the side of the road. Then, they open the trunk and continue their morning routine like combing their hair and stepping out of their PJs. This is when we see that they had transformed the back seat of the car into an improvised bed for two. On top of the car, they have a cargo box where they store everything and a bike rack on the trunk door. I guess you can travel only by car, always having your own place to sleep. This is how they miss nothing, including the wild buffalos grazing outside their bedroom.

We carry on with our trip, talking about the recent encounter and the makeshift motorhome the couple improvised to make up for their lack of financial resources. M. tells me this is something common. Many people, who cannot afford either an RV or the accommodations, alter three-quarters of their car or van and travel wherever they want. There are plenty of truck stops where you can shower for a few quarters, so hygiene can be under control while living in your car.

Five coffee sips later, we entered the park. We present the pass to the same amiable staff, receive the map, local paper, and greetings for a wonderful day. Then, we head to the Grand Canyon Lodge to park the car. What follows next is an amazing story about a resort that is too good to be rooted in reality.

Starting from the parking lot, we pass small and large cabins emplaced through the woods that seam the canyon's edge and leave me speechless. All of them are built out of long sturdy logs, with decorative stone, tall windows with dark green frames. Two rocking chairs rest on each shaded porch. I imagine what a dream it would be to sleep so close to the canyon, drinking my coffee sitting in a rocking chair, gazing at the pine forest, saying hello to all the visitors walking by my porch and wishing them a great day.

I don't get to entertain this fantasy for very long, because my imagination has to take a more elaborate test when we face the canyon at the North Rim Grand Canyon Lodge, built ninety years ago.

I do not know what first catches my eye, the lodge or the canyon, but I am certain that for a fraction of a second, my heart skips a beat. Although I want to articulate many onomatopoeias of delight, the vowels and consonants are piling up in my throat, preventing me from harmoniously grouping them together. I guess it is better this way, because the view lying before my eyes deserves infinitely more than my vocalizations.

The first impression is that the Grand Canyon is anything but grand. It is colossal, astronomical, herculean, monumental, titanic. It cannot be contained in a glance and, as soon as it enters your visual area, the eyes are constantly trying to figure out the pattern Nature used when creating this work of art. I wish I could produce extra words just to express my awe for this massive stone sculpture!

The Grand Canyon is a world in itself, which has remained untouched for millions of years, imposing and capable of leaving you tongue-tied. You can only stare and behold its endless contours, rummaging through your vocabulary for epithets and metaphors. You might have seen images and footage of the horizonless gorge of the Colorado River and think it was only fair to be declared a UNESCO[3] heritage. However, when you see it live, you wish Theodore Roosevelt had also been awarded the Nobel, the Oscar, and the Pulitzer Prize too, in the acclaim of the yearly five million visitors.

It is not the largest or the longest river on the North American continent. But from the Rocky Mountains to the Gulf of California, the Colorado River leaves behind a calligraphy comprehended probably only by aliens when looking over the vast land. Its waters have been digging so deep into the Colorado Plateau for millions of years that it is simply impossible for me to understand what it looked like in the beginning. The banks are hundreds of feet high, narrow at the base and wider toward the top until they measure tens of miles between them.

I envision a giant honey-pecan-pistachio-mille-feuille, randomly eaten by intergalactic colossuses, uncovering never-ending layers of the cinnamon-dusted dessert.

We stick around the lodge's large terrace facing the vastness of the canyon. I gradually regained most of my senses and started manifesting the desire of taking selfies with M. and the fabulous background, just like so many other families and couples near us. My traveler's habits kick in, as it always happens with all the firsts on this trip, when I need to discover and learn as much as possible about the beauty before me.

We take landscape and portrait pictures, zoom in or out photos and videos, with or without us at their center. The day is beautiful and the clear sky unveils the wooded south rim, with its diminutive and dense plants. All the canyons I will visit from now on have their unique, arbitrary patterns of a charming and wild allure.

I am still on the deck, fantasizing about sweet and savory culinary comparisons, when I notice an adorable senior couple comfortably settled in Adirondack chairs, each of them holding a cup of coffee. I also see a container of sliced fruit laid between the two on the wide armrest. They seem to be used to the scenery, because, at some point, the woman takes a book out of her bag and starts reading. This picture mesmerizes me, and I stealthily photograph the silky-white-haired woman who chose the most fantastic place on earth for reading. Now and then, she takes a break from the story, which I hope is just as overwhelming as the backdrop of her leisure activity, and discretely asks the tourists if they want her to help them take a photo of the entire family. She is very successful and nobody refuses her. How could anybody say no to her? This way, the granny from the fairy tale creates permanent portraits for exotic language-speaking foreigners with the old canyon in the background.

I sigh with a silly smile on my face, truly touched by the

human beauty, and carry on with my research. Oh, yes, the lodge! A place as special as the Grand Canyon deserved to have an imposing building for a sentinel, and those who designed it seem to have had the same exact intention.

Propped upright on the edge of the canyon, tall thick logs and massive beige-reddish stone walls assemble its profile. I pop in the building with magnifying-glass-eyes and memory recording mode on. As if it were not enough that nature wrote the screenplay for a National Geographic documentary outside these walls, man has pledged a matching trophy inside.

They call the main entrance The Sunroom, the first one that the visitors see when entering the lodge, the kind of living room used as a common space. Compared to what I have seen lodge-related so far, this seems more like the whole thing, not just a room. I notice the rock walls, probably thirty feet tall, the stairs and banisters painted in dark brown, an old piano, a sculpture representing a donkey sitting on its rear—an homage to the thousands of donkeys carrying tourists along the riverbed. There is also an educative section of the Colorado Plateau made of what seems painted plaster, showing the first fifteen layers of the earth's crust, devoured by water since the era of the dinosaurs.

What captures my attention and stays imprinted upon my retina are the three windows - around 250 square feet wide each, with wooden frames, through which the light invades the room unhindered, along with the still image of the canyon. This is where it probably gained its name. Nine brown leather sofas and some akin armchairs lie strategically grouped facing the exposed nature, like in the cinema.

A few visitors, immersed in the folds of the sofas, lose themselves in the scenery. Others are having breakfast in the restaurant next door, and I am utterly amazed at what a real lodge means in these parts of the world.

I could stay here until sundown. Across from the comfortable sofas and beyond the glass windows, the sun has been setting every day for millions of years. It would be enough for me to see only that. Just being on the sunny terrace or in the Sunroom would be fulfilling. Honestly, I am not fussy. However, there are so many trails to hike and vistas to visit. The day is so unfairly short that I tear my sight away from the wide windows and think to myself that no matter where we go, we will still be in the middle of striking places.

I will never forget that out of the tens of picturesque trails going through or around the canyon, we chose one meant for horseback riding tours. Three miles of trail covered in sand and manure, half downhill and half uphill, discovered and named after a certain Uncle Jim.

It makes little sense to us why this trail is unlike the others until groups of tourists mounted on different four-legged traction animals with no humps get ahead of us. It becomes even clearer after they congratulate us on undertaking the trail with no means of transportation. Now we are sure we could have chosen a trek that would not change the color of our shoes and load them with half a pound of sand each, but it is all the same to us considering where we are.

We get to cross a secular forest inhabited by break-dancing squirrels and chipmunks, decorated with plants and flowers perfect for an A+ herbarium, wrapped in clear blue skies, breathable temperature, and surprise: a restroom halfway through the loop! I would say it is a perfect hike, considering that the twenty ounces of coffee I have drunk are sharpening my senses.

At the end of the trail, we forget about the heavy and uncomfortable boots, but we will probably remember them on our way back. For a while, though, we are only aware of the fact that spectacular landscapes are difficult to come by. We are on the brim of the canyon, up above boundless ravines that flow one from another along the zigzagged green river bed.

It is just us here, the sole spectators of a premiere show. That is, if we do not count the middle-aged couple from Florida who are about to leave as we arrive. As usual, we make some small talk about where we are from, what we have been visiting, and where we are heading after, just like on any other trail. We say goodbye to them and climb the most peripheral cliff, one that my mother would certainly not let me climb if she saw me, but one that offers the most spectacular views. We are above one of the world's wonders, admiring its splendor, listening to its ceaseless motion, inhaling the smell of vigorous nature, and memorizing the moment for the rest of our lives.

Afterward, we cover the entire itinerary proposed by the park handout, this time with the conveyance. We stop at every vista point and take everything in. At the first one with a picnic area, we have our lunch with the canyon in the background. It might be another gathering of all the vegetables from the cooler into a disposable bowl kind of lunch, crammed under three types of cheese and drowned in ranch dressing, but it is a special lunch, just like the entire day.

With the sunset warming the backs of our heads, we return to camp. The same forest is there but without the buffalos this time. We both think of something that impressed us during the day but words are in vain. We enjoy the silence while our faces speak as much as a chapter in this book.

The tent is still there. Nobody found it attractive enough to take it down and steal it. It's not that we expected something like this to happen. OK, maybe just for a split second out of habit.

We fix ourselves dinner out of the same ingredients we had for the last four meals. Anyway, who's counting when you are at high altitude and far away from the mountains of fries, brisket, and BBQ sauce? We have quite an appetite and eat the contents of the bowl along with all the crumbs on the table. Then we get ready for another night in the middle of the wilderness.

I try to freshen up as much as possible in a no-plumbing camping restroom and say thank you for the wet wipes. I then politely wait for my turn to brush my teeth by the water pump, while a man is filling up a bucket. After just a few minutes of waiting, I found out that his name is Bosko, he is of Serbian descent, lives in Arizona, and he vacations here every summer with his brother and parents. He finds out just as much about M. and I, which is standard socializing between strangers in the States.

By a water pump. In a campground. We say goodbye with the warmest wishes and the promise that we will not miss the Coral Pink Sand Dunes on our way to Zion National Park.

The night passes faster this time. I used up all the bloody scenes where bears feast on me for dinner, and I am too tired to make up new ones. There is no more strength left in my bones to squirm around whenever I hear a rustle near the bright-orange tent. I am burned out, because walking on sand for hours is nothing like an afternoon nap. So, I fall asleep without a chance to play the victim.

# 11 - *ANTELOPE CANYON, AZ ☼ CORAL PINK SAND DUNES, KANAB, LA VERKIN, UT*

**M**ornings are so wonderful in the campground. That is, unless it has been raining, or a bear has snacked on a tourist overnight, of course. There is blue in the sky, coolness in the air, and dew on every green thing. The tents and RVs seem to be all in place. Same number as last night. I am still sleepy as the sun barely creeps through the jammed pine trunks of the forest. We leave in record time, because it turns out that M. and I are a highly efficient leisure equipment packing-unpacking mechanism. Plus, we skip breakfast as the menu we have been munching on has reached the climax of boredom.

We stopped by Meadow's Edge, the small convenience store outside the campground, to pump some gas, fill the cooler with ice and my mug with coffee. Although all these actions are straightforward and doable in less than five moves per person, we discover that M. and I are also a forgetful and giddy mechanism at times, when each of us thinks of something very different.

M. worries that it is already late and that we will miss the Antelope Canyon tour. Our next destination. I too am a bit restless, as the barista from the trailer-turned-coffee shop has just woken up. It will surely take some time until I will leave coffee-handed. After a short moment of panic when M. believes he has locked the keys inside the car, and we do the math on how long it will take for the dealership to send us a spare key; and after an even shorter moment when we discover that the car is, in fact, unlocked, we are on our way. However, when we open the cooler to grab a bottle of water, we notice that the salad box is missing; thus, we conclude we left it on the top of the car when we filled up the cooler with ice. Looks like we are not the only ones sick of salad. The salad was also sick of us.

M. and all the tourist guides in the West say that you haven't seen Arizona until you visit Antelope Canyon. Which we do. At mile 4,271, on the canicular 1st of July 2018. At 11:45 am, we park the car, apply generous amounts of sunscreen on our already tanned exposed skin, grab a bottle of water and head to the tribal booking office to pick up the tickets M. bought over two months ago.

We are once again in Navajo Land, a highly popular place managed by the native tribe. Lower Antelope Canyon can only be visited through a guided tour. But, because of the summer crowds, you can only save a spot by booking it one season in advance.

It is a photographer's paradise. They say that the secret of taking the best shots is to visit the canyon midday when the sunlight penetrates perpendicularly through the slot canyon walls creating yellow-orange laser-like rays. We are not professionals but insist on visiting this gorge at the right time to see it in all of its glory. Who knows? Maybe we will actually take home some spectacular photos of its astounding shapes and colors.

Next to the ticket office, there is an improvised outdoor covered waiting area where visitors take shelter from the torrid sun, awaiting their turn to tour. Some sit on benches, some stand, but all seem happy to be in the shade away from the 105°F heat. But I guess you could still get a nice tan even here in the shade. Regardless, we pick a spot as far as possible from the direct sunlight just to be cautious.

The organizers provide entertainment for their guests by offering them an authentic and complete experience. While waiting for the tour, a Native American man, dressed up in traditional Navajo attire, dances and juggles with eight hula-hoops and the skills of an America's Got Talent contestant. But hold on! During the audience's applause, the man confesses that he made it to the final of the aforementioned show with the same artistic movements.

At noon on the dot, Andrea the guide, gathers the fourteen people on the list, introduces herself, and shortly narrates the history of the Navajo Canyon *The place where water runs through rocks*. Unlike the Grand Canyon, which is the Colorado River's doing, Antelope Canyon, like all the other slot canyons in the American West, is a result of flooding.

This plateau of Navajo sandstone is, as its name implies, sandy. Yes, we are in the desert, and it is hot and dry. However, during the monsoon season, the water mixed with sand travels with unimagined speed through the walls flooding the slot canyon and forming the waves of stone for which it is so famous. Amazingly, the downpours happen tens of miles away from here.

The Navajo sandstone is a brick-red color, but because of the water friction and the sand transported by it in a whirling flow, the walls mimic the shape of the ocean waves and the random color of the sand. After descending into the belly of the canyon on sturdy abrupt metal stairs, Andrea shows explicitly how this landform was born using a small pile of sand and a bottle of water.

We follow the guide one behind the other, a group of fourteen followed by another group and so on, passing at a slow pace through this underground geography that resembles the stomach of a whale. The amazement springs from all around, and interjections pop up in all the languages of the world.

We photograph almost every curve, as they seem so different from one another, aquatic shapes and pastel tones so masterfully mixed by an eccentric artist. The light is the key element here, as the sunbeams pervade the tight slits of the ceiling, sharpening or fading the colors, giving the canyon a psychedelic effect. If you have a professional camera and know how to use it, you can take fantastic pictures, especially now, when the sun is perpendicular and the rays appear as incandescent spears stabbing the gulch.

The arched walls that contort here and there seem to be made of caramel, or candied honey mixed with moist crème brûlée molded with a spoon by the same aliens who were satisfying their hunger in the Grand Canyon the other day. We try to follow directions about the aperture, shutter speed, and ISO that Andrea dictates every time we reach another breathtaking curve. At least in theory, the images would guarantee works of photographic art. But my clumsiness succeeds only in capturing the shadows instead of the light, as I am to discover later when I will have downloaded everything on my laptop. Still, with all the technological failures, we take a few portraits with us, modest yet faithful to the unearthly surroundings, using only the automatic features of the camera. With or without the sunshine piercing through the air while translucent sand particles float all over, we will still overwhelm my mother with our photos.

As we get closer to the end of the hike, we ask some of our tour colleagues to take photos of us together. At one point, we hear, *"Frumos, nu-i aşa?[4]"* coming from somewhere behind our group. Yes, in the heart of the state of Arizona, we met our first fellow citizen. She is a Romanian woman from Moldova married to an American. They came from Oregon to visit the ins and outs of the Navajo Land and Colorado Plateau. We wish each other safe travels, then take a photo with Andrea while noticing the torrent of people waiting to take their turn inside the canyon. Afterwards, we are on our way to the place Bosko, the Serbian, recommended to us the other day.

Since many of the local attractions are in the same area between Utah and Arizona, we oscillate from one state to another, according to M.'s elaborate plan. At mile 4,295 we reenter Utah and take a detour to see the sets of some movies my mother must have watched at least twice as they were filmed between 1942 and 1972: *Mackenna's Gold, Ali Baba* and T*he Forty Thieves* and *Arabian Nights.* Just to name a few.

Coral Pink Sand Dunes is one of the state parks in Utah that compete with all the others, relying on the unlikely existence of dunes in the middle of nowhere. Coming from Kanab, tall dunes rise out of the background on the left side of the road, colored in coral. It is just as improbable ever getting to see such a thing as it would be to find a permanent glacier here.

Navajo sandstone is yet again to blame for this unusual manifestation of nature. Having as accomplices the Moquith and Moccasin Mountains, the wind that blows among them faster than Rafael Nadal[5]'s serve, has been successfully hauling sand onto this plateau through the Venturi effect. Bit by bit, enough sand piled up to border the shores of the Black Sea with fine pink sand.

In the end, all nature's embodiments have a scientific explanation for their origin. It is not my intention to take the fun out of some amazing dunes and break them down to technicalities. No, I put on my hiking shoes and set out across the dunes, far behind M. and his long stork-like-legs that help him walk on the sand as if it were asphalt. It is not as easy for me. I'm not complaining, just advancing intentionally slowly, taking in the scene.

It would be ideal to walk barefoot on the sand. I know. It would be romantic, even without the ocean waves, but we insist on keeping our soles intact. If the outside temperature is over 105°F, the sand can easily replace a hot stove. Indeed, our shoes are rather like ladles we rummage through the sand with, but at least there is a protective layer between the stove and the skin. Although the soles of our boots might thin out by the end of the walk. I speak from experience when I say that walking on sand is an exhausting business, just as it was on Uncle Jim's trail in the Grand Canyon. Therefore, I prefer sitting on top of a dune (after having dug out a substantial bed of sand and reaching a cooler layer) while M. ventures to the next dunes.

I draw a few sand angels because I can't help myself, then I cover my legs with sand and pretend to be a mermaid for a couple of hot seconds. I gather sand in my palms and let it slip through my fingers like an hourglass. I look at my hands in the sunlight and notice that the sand particles turn to gold.

M. comes back, just as nimble as he left, and tells me that the dunes go on farther than he imagined. I believe him. We head back to the parking lot, crossing paths with groups of visitors mounted on motorcycles and buggies. I bet this entire experience could get far more pleasant riding one of those.

At mile 4,358 we breeze into Kanab, a small desert mountain town, a place where M. seems to feel at home. He tells me, with a smile in his eyes and profound devotion, that he knows by heart every street, restaurant, and hotel. This is where he spent most nights on his previous mountain vacations, being so close to Zion, his favorite park.

Kanab is the winner of the strategic location contest, as it lies in the Grand Circle, between the main attractions of Arizona and Utah: Vermilion Cliffs National Monument, Bryce Canyon National Park, the Grand Canyon (North Rim), Zion National Park, Lake Powell, Grand Staircase-Escalante National Monument, and Coral Pink Sand Dunes State Park. M. is so happy to be here again, and I am so lucky to visit this entire region even once. Some of these sites are new to M. as well. Therefore, from now on, what follows for about a week will be valuable writing material for me.

We have lunch and a mojito at Rocking V Café, then cross the entire Zion valley. I stare out the window, and point my finger when I spot a mountain that looks like a chessboard, two tunnels with wide arches cut out where secret landscapes and waterfalls show their wonder, and a mother hiking up a trail with her baby in a pouch. Leaving Zion a few days later, I learned that they call the mountain in question Checkerboard Mesa.

We will be back in Zion in two days, and then we will have the chance to know each other a lot better. Right now, we are heading to La Verkin, where we'll spend the next four nights. We could have taken a faster route, but M. will not say no to any opportunity to bathe his eyes in the park's tall mountains, hiding the most abrupt and impressive canyons.

Leaving the valley, we enter Springdale, a real mountain resort. I have seen nothing like this before, just like all the places that keep showing up in front of me ever since we left Gilberts, Illinois. Indeed, I haven't visited many mountain resorts in my life, except for Predeal and Sinaia[6] in the Carpathians, but one can't compare Springdale to them. It is clean and flirtatious, with art galleries, cactus bordered sidewalks, lodges, mountain gear shops, and restaurants built out of brown and red painted logs. There are neat white bridges over the Virgin River, sweetshops and ice cream parlors, large terraces crowded with people from all over the world, of all ages and colors. The streets are lined with houses painted in light tones and freshly mowed front lawns. Some of them have blue pools or ponds. Exiting the resort, I notice extensive areas designated for horseback riding.

In about twenty minutes, at mile 4,436, we reach the La Verkin Best Western Hotel, our host for the next few days. We take our luggage up to room 317 and finish the day washing out the sand we unintentionally stole at noon, now stuck under our armpits and between our toes.

# CHAPTER V - *UTAH, LIFE ELEVATED*

# 12 - *WHITE POCKET, VERMILION CLIFFS NATURAL MONUMENT, AZ* ☼ *COYOTE WASH, BUCKSKIN GULCH, UT*

I t is a much-anticipated day for both of us. We plan to visit the White Pocket, which will be a first, even for M. Our excursion will be a logistical challenge for obvious reasons: only a portion of the road is paved and the rest is covered in sand and completely unmarked. We put our trust in our 4-wheel drive Subaru rental and feel quite uneasy at the possibility of being stuck in the sand. So far away from civilization. I'm not worried though, mostly because I am the passenger, and also because I trust M.'s driving skills and reflexes. Moreover, he has been researching for days. He watched videos of other tourists attempting to visit White Pocket and caught a glimpse of what the road looks like. We have Google Maps on our side too but don't know yet how much it will help us.

We experience a complete range of emotions until we reach the white stone pockets that we insist on seeing up close, not just in photos. Luckily, it all ends well because of M.'s sharp instincts.

Chronologically, we first enter a rough unpaved road, then a sandy one-way road, with unexpectedly large rocks hidden under the sand. The car's belly hits loudly some of the rocks, which makes M. curse bilingually. All around there is the same typical desert, only this time big gray hares jump left and right, exotic blue birds seem to fly out of birdcages and hostile low vegetation with stiff branches scratch at the car doors.

After a few miles, we realize that this is not the road shown in the YouTube videos. It's missing a gate. We turn around to the unpaved rough road that leads us further to another one just as sandy as the first one, but that has White Pocket at the end of it.

We encounter another car parked near the only sign in tens of miles, and one small panel from the National Conservation Lands showing this is a Vermilion Cliffs Natural Monument. I am puzzled to find such an unmarked place in a country where it's practically impossible to get lost. Yet it makes sense. The authorities protect it with no effort and only the truly determined visitors will make it here.

When we had lunch the other day at Rock V Café in Kanab, I saw a framed poster that read *"White Pocket, Like the Wave, but without the lottery."* Most natural monuments preserved in the United States are no longer accessible to the public but only to a few fortunate ones. At the beginning of every year, The Bureau of Land Management organizes a lottery for exploring the fantastic Wave and offers only twenty entries per day. No matter the season, M. applied in the past and also last year, but without luck. The same thing happens to thousands of other tourists, but those who are more informed know that White Pocket is the younger sibling of the Wave and don't regret losing the lottery.

At the beginning of this year, M. took his chances with a few emblematic natural monuments such as the Wave, Havasu Falls (known as the paradise waterfalls in the heart of the Navajo reservation in Arizona), and the Subway (the spectacular exit of Left-Fork North Creek through its canyon in Zion National Park, perfectly resembling a subway opening). With a success rate of 33.3%, M. won a single lottery. For July 4, nonetheless.

We are at peace with the limited amount of luck we had for the drawing of lots, because we are as we speak entering White Pocket. Our mouths are already full of exclamations, and our eyes are swallowing the landscape whole. If it is anything like the Wave, it is because this is the exact impression you have getting here. You are like a surfer keeping your balance on top of foamy waves on an ocean of stone.

I understand that here too the time and weather have been conspiring for millions of years against the rocks, but how they shaped it into such a lively and unsteady appearance is beyond my capacity to comprehend. What I am able to do is enjoy this serene day, walk on the stiff shore of this colorful Navajo sandstone mountain, and inhale its beauty. Then imprint it in this book in a torrent of cheering to this miraculous planet we have the chance to live on.

We go up on white froth peaks and down in dark red valleys, under stone arches that resemble the parabolic contour of a wave right before breaking. We mirror ourselves in the leftover waters of the last rains, in the shade of the cliffs. We cross sand patches where thorny cacti show their round ears. Then land on a wide dale that makes me think of the milky crème of a cappuccino in which a barista artistically blended a splash of cocoa and cinnamon, and then added scoops of vanilla and walnut ice cream on the side.

Every step of the way, we are tempted to steal the image of these fantastic contorted stones into our cameras, because being here seems surreal. Later though, watching how the screen will loyally restore reality, it might be easier for us to realize that July 2, 2018 existed, and that we spent it under the sky of a faraway corner of the world called White Pocket.

John Fowles[7] believed that nature is constantly changing, while painting and photography fossilize it, keeping it captive in the past as it once had been. I agree with that. However, it is not the case here. A landscape where the natural elements are short-lived, like the freshness of my complexion, is in danger of becoming unrecognizable from spring until fall. But here, these stones needed millions of years to change their curves, so my photos will be up-to-date for many centuries to come.

My day may as well end here, maybe even the week, and everything we have already experienced would be enough. But when it rains, it pours fortune and exuberance for us. It is not even lunchtime yet, and we have another exotic destination on our list. I'm embodying gratefulness, even though from time to time someone has to pinch me to make sure I am aware of my whereabouts. I am living the dream of traveling. A dream so many people have. I am the traveler I imagined, tracing dots on a map of a world too big for me to become familiar with. But M. offered me the chance of becoming a bit more acquainted with what it feels like living in a dream.

We barely find our way back to the car, as the only sign is right next to it. Therefore, it takes a while to circle back, walking around the long stone shore, surrounded by a sea of sand tinted by dark green shrubs, and eventually reuniting with our car. Nothing worries us. Not this, anyway. However, the thought of having to drive back to the asphalt, on the same deep sandy road as this morning, takes on a completely new perspective when we spot in the distance the shiny windshield of our brave car.

There are a couple of other cars parked next to ours, but we have not met their owners on our hike. We had the distinct impression that we were the only ones in the middle of the stone monument.

It is not just us on the way back either. Halfway to civilization we have to go around an abandoned car that is stuck in the red sand. It is not just that there are no signs, but there is no network either. So, the driver must be looking for cellphone reception to call somebody for help. The unhappy situation the car is in shocks us, as it is more robust than ours is. In sandy conditions such as this, salvation depends on the driver. M. knows exactly how to approach the land's instability under the wheels and lands us right on the road to the Buckskin Gulch, the longest slot canyon in the world.

There is no entrance kiosk in the parking lot before the trailhead, nor a cute ranger sticking his head out of the window while checking our pass and wishing us a glorious day. Here, we found a self-pay-station. It looks like a mailbox where visitors supposedly have to drop the $6/person fee together with their contact info so that the authorities can later issue them a receipt. I am so curious how many of them pay the park entrance fee. Leaving the payment up to the visitors is not something I am used to. I find this act of trust from the authorities quite remarkable.

It's noon, and the sun follows our every move, hovering above our heads. We wet the buffs in the icy cold cooler water before putting them on. We wear them in a legionnaire style, stretching them from our eyebrows to the back of our heads. We apply several ounces of sunscreen on portions of our skin that already have a well-baked bread color, fill up the backpack with water bottles, and off we go towards Buckskin Gulch.

Up to the canyon entrance, there are about three miles of hiking through the Coyote Wash, a trail entirely covered in red Navajo stone sand. Even though I gave up verbally expressing my utter antipathy for the July desert climate, I have to mention that the vigilant sun shoots at us 104°F sunrays. As used as I might have gotten by now to its hot treatment, I never ignore a patch of shade under a stuck-out crag or a tall enough plant.

A break of even a few minutes can cool me down and energize me for another mile. However, the thought of being rewarded with an abundance of shade once we are in the gulch makes me bear the remaining miles with a contagious liveliness.

A genuine surprise is the Wire Pass we cross right before entering the main canyon where we find unlimited coolness. It's shady between the wide tall walls, which makes me feel safe.

Buckskin Gulch, with its fifteen-mile length, is the longest and deepest slot canyon in the world. A geological wonder. But it is also one of the most dangerous hikes if approached during the wrong season. Like Antelope Canyon and many others in this area, the gulch inherited its present anatomy from the high floods that have been digging into the Colorado Plateau for millions of years. Tree trunks flung by the torrents and stuck athwart between the walls, prove the rage and speed the water possessed when sculpting this landmark, and how risky it would be to find yourself in its midst at the wrong time.

We are safe exploring the canyon during this hot dry summer though. Still, if we were here during any other time of the year, we would have a bleak fate walking at the bottom of these abrupt walls if a downpour would happen even tens of miles away. In a few minutes, the whole valley would flood. There are no other exits, except for the two at opposite ends, fifteen miles apart. Wherever we would find ourselves inside the gulch, there would be no escape for us. Even if we tried our best to climb the mostly overhanging walls.

There is no reason for me to worry about being in this steep valley created by floods and bordered left and right by stone shores as high as 500 feet in places. Especially not when I see M. hopping with delight that he finally made it to this famous canyon.

I understand his enthusiasm, and for at least one more mile, I am more impressed than terrified. When we stumble upon portions of dried or rather petrified mud, looking like baking chocolate broken into forty-pound pieces, I realize how much water was necessary to create these craters and how hopeless I would be if they were in liquid form right now. Soon after this, my state of mind shifts, and all I want is to see myself safely returned to the car, wet mostly from sweat.

The way back is always harder for me. Physically, I mean. The incredible energy of the places I make my own, one by one, with efforts I rarely feel capable of, overwhelm my spirit with a new fresh zest for life and gives me enough endurance to bring myself back unharmed.

Buckskin Gulch is a torrid and untamed memory, and the simple fact that I crossed it, even for a few miles, shows me I have been becoming a more curious and increasingly patient human being. Nature is capable of such deeds: wake people up from their civilized dreams and make them face the essence of the earth that hosts them. It is, probably, the most efficient slap in the face that could ever open one's eyes to what is truly important in life.

Wrapped in grateful thoughts, I comfortably lay in bed next to M. Every night around this hour, he downloads maps and plans the next day. I fell asleep watching us spoon in a king-size bed somewhere far away, in a spacious hotel room in La Verkin, Utah, surrounded by hundreds of miles of desert. As I distance myself from the bedsheets and encompass more and more of the big picture, we become smaller and smaller until we are one tiny grain of Navajo sand swallowed by this endless country.

# 13 - *ZION NATIONAL PARK, KANARRA FALLS, UT*

About twenty miles from the little town that has been hosting us for the last two nights, stands Zion National Park, the one we crossed the other day. We will return there today, M. probably for the tenth time. Oh, if you could just see how happy M. is to be back here. You would say he is a fish that has just dived back into water after a long break on dry land. Because we will spend only one day here, M. chose the Observation Point for us to hike, the highest destination in the entire Zion valley, in its entire green and young splendor.

Again, we have to start as early as possible, because although we are practically in the mountains, we are also in the desert. (I know, it is quite hard to understand how that is possible, but it is.) The heat is just as strong here as it was at lower altitudes. And it would be smart to hike the most troublesome part on the way up in the shade.

The whole dynamic of the park is extraordinarily laid out, starting with the infrastructure. Zion-Mount Carmel Highway cuts the park in two from east to west and unites Springdale to the State Road 89, the only car accessible way to the park. From South to North, there is a special route created to offer access to the main Zion attractions, where transportation is free and electric shuttles carry the public from dawn until dusk. Private automobiles would clutter this pass and make it impracticable considering the thousands of daily visitors; therefore, they are banned from entering this valley.

The Zion shuttle has about fifteen stops where visitors politely wait in line, hop on in the order of their arrival, respecting the limit imposed by the driver, who must keep in mind the people waiting at the next stops. There is no hurry because buses come every ten minutes. Bus stops are strategically dispersed along the valley, easing the gateway to all the trailheads. Obviously, people here have never crowded into a Cluj-Napoca[8] (the fourth largest city in Romania) trolley around 7 pm on a Thursday in the fall. To me, it is extremely unusual, but a pleasure, to find that people can board the bus in a civilized manner.

M. knows his way around. So, we leave the car in the parking lot and walk to the second stop, as the first one has at least a hundred well-equipped and eager visitors in the queue. It is unbelievable how many people are here, of all ages and ethnicities, who come to enjoy a few days outdoors. I have seen nothing like this back home except for experienced mountaineers hiking the Carpathians and individuals who consider grilling sausages at the forest's edge a quality time spent in nature. Therefore, I am so pleased to see families with children and gray-haired grandparents enjoying a short hike. There are young people with backpacks full of harnesses, ropes, bolts, and carabiners who take on the challenge of climbing cliffs or descending into dark deep canyons (M. would fit in this category, but with me by his side, he gratefully declines the canyoneer status). In addition, there are others just like me, surviving gracefully on intermediate treks. There is obvious demand for this type of recreational activity in the States and here is the supply.

We hustled to the second station, where less than eight tourists were waiting in line. We will board the next bus for sure. We rode for about ten minutes. In another ten, we are at the trailhead, with our laces tied and backpacks full of water and snacks. For the moment, we are at the foot of Baldy Mountain, but in approximately four miles of abrupt switchbacks, a rather strenuous hike, we will be on top of it, ruling over the still shady valley.

We are not the only ones gathering their courage to face the mountain wall. Well, it's mostly I who needs encouragement, because for M. this is like a relaxing walk on a beach at sunset. Here is where all the visitors that don't climb up to Angel's Landing come, a panoramic place that entails a shorter hike and a less steep trail.

As usual, without even acknowledging it, M. makes me surpass my athletic abilities. Somehow, flattered by his trust, I just jumped headfirst into the wild American map. Until now, I handled all the challenges, which made me grow in my own eyes and fill my chest with such pride, if not conceit. But it was never easy. Just as I sensed it won't be this time either.

For two-and-a-half miles, there are constant abrupt angled switchbacks. After maybe twenty of them, I realize I can't ascend them like M. (one after the other, whistling and admiring the scenery), without challenging my heart and muscles. So, I hike three or four at a time. Then, I rest for a minute, until I catch my breath and restore my thoracic capacity and can confront the next switchback. My strategy works like magic, although from time to time, I have to adjust the frequencies of the stops or break minutes. Regardless, I march up the mountain at quite a nice pace, often passing groups of tourists that breathlessly decide that they can only do it by taking breaks after each curve.

Agile slender Zion squirrels, arrogant and immune to the gravitational force, animate the short trees bordering the path. On a sloping canyon wall, covered with gravel and tangled dry roots, a beautiful big horn mountain sheep is taking its morning stroll, ignoring any laws of balance. If I look closely, it reminds me of M.

The last mile and a half are mild, with flat areas in places and a crescendo at the end, through Echo Canyon. Still, I try to do my best as I go up, remembering the moment I concluded I can conquer this summit. Everybody around me looks burned-out, just like me, except for M., of course, who is probably bored with waiting for me to catch up with him. I look back to the trail behind me and decide that it was worth every sweat drop and every muscle cramp, because, finally, we are on top of the world at Observation Point in Zion!

This is it! No more whining. Here, there is only room for an exclamation of admiration. Honestly, I have already forgotten how I landed here. All I know is that I am in an overwhelmingly beautiful place. My only regret is that my sight is not 360 degrees wide to contain everything at a glance. Taking in every little corner of this spectacular view is more like an engorging than a passive contemplation. But, I am not the only one unable to determine what to look at first. Most of the people who made it this far have ecstatic faces, just like mine that give this place a contagious positive energy. M. knows this spot by heart, and he stands out as one of the regulars.

The serene deep blue sky dilutes gradually towards the horizon and the translucid moon hangs over the Zion valley like a precious ornament on the Christmas tree. Pine forests style the flat tops of the cliffs, and long-eared spiky cacti and tousled shrubs decorate the vertical walls of the canyon, tinting the red and beige of the stone with a little green. From up here, the dale resembles a river of greenery winding between rocky banks, as we stand on the upper deck of a gigantic cruise ship.

We sat down close to the edge of the butte, each of us on a boulder so well polished by the millions of rear-ends that ever sat on them throughout the history of the park. We hydrate and snack while actively taking part in the dynamic of this place. We fall in love with the landscape and enjoy watching the reactions of the newcomers. Next, we take lots of pictures, selfies, *usies*[9], and family portraits when asked by our fellow travelers with fresh amazement on their faces. I could do this for the rest of the day, without getting bored, but the local entertainment just gets more attractive.

A few chipmunks show up on stage searching for brunch. These are Uinta Chipmunks. A species that only lives here in Zion. I am sure you know what I'm talking about, because you watched them on TV throughout your childhood in Disney cartoons. Chip and Dale, those restless tiny creatures always foraging, who constantly give Donald Duck a hard time. In Romanian, we call them squirrels with large jaws or striped squirrels. They don't have their own word, because there aren't any of them in Eastern Europe. They are nonetheless chipmunks, and from here on, I find them all over the place in the mountain-desert areas. They have many subtle variations of colors and the number of stripes they have on their backs and tails varies as well. They are just adorable. These creatures and their unexpected apparition won me over for good!

They are small and delicate, resembling sparrows with fur that do not fly but are extremely agile and have an amazing speed in movements that exceeds my ability to follow them. I would say they suffer from ADHD, but without being affected by the attention deficit, which makes them notice something edible from considerable distances. This is pretty much what they do all day.

They are reasonably polite and don't throw themselves at the food once they spot it, but wait patiently to be offered a crumb; if not offered, they just mind their own business and search for new targets. People really should not feed them, because this is how they become dependent on humans and lose their ability to be self-sufficient.

As M.'s backpack is lying on the ground, Chip or Dale, not sure which, climbs it and inspects it thoroughly. Then it goes on M.'s leg up to his knee, obviously being attracted to the banana peel he ostentatiously holds in his hand. Apparently, I don't care as much about the wildlife diet, because I throw a piece of apple its way. It grabs it cautiously, making sure its peers haven't noticed, turns its back to the mesmerized public, and starts nibbling on it at a speed known only by Disney's characters.

As we prepare to head back, we take some photos of our new friends and then start descending. I imagine the four miles back will be a piece of cake for me, and I will pace them like a little girl who has just received a plush chipmunk from Santa Claus. (I know. I too notice all the comparisons to a little girl made throughout this book and it only goes to show that my experiences have been genuine.) Instead of hopping, my joints, my ankles, and knees squeak like a rusted bike, and my toes press against the top of the boots as if they want to turn them into sandals.

All the same, I make it downhill in one piece, with the boots intact and acute pain in my bones and leg muscles. Finding myself at the flat bus stop, I ignore every discomfort and give in to M.'s praises and compliments. M. had known all along that I could do this hike; therefore, he was once again right. He really enjoys being right.

At this early hour, there isn't a return queue, so we embus the first shuttle that comes with plenty of available seats. As it is a lot less crowded and quieter than this morning, we can hear the funny woman driver abusing the supplied microphone:

*"Now leaving Weeping Rock stop, number seven on your maps, and heading next to The Grotto stop, where you can access Kayenta Trail, West Rim Trail, or Angel's Landing. In this hot weather, you should get off the bus at the next stop, at the Zion Lodge, and hike up to the Emerald Pools and cool off by the waterfalls or in one of the natural pools. If I were you, I would buy a big ice cream and enjoy it sitting on the grass, under the shady trees in front of the Visitor Center. Either way, hydrate, use sun lotion, use hiking poles, if possible, and take lots of pictures!"*

I truly appreciate the open and friendly discussion with the tourists. It is a manifestation of hospitality that makes me feel welcome, which I have encountered nowhere back home in any circumstances. From the start, I sensed the locals' selfless warmth, and they somehow infected me with it. Just think of it: it costs nothing to be nice to others, and the effort is minimal. Take the driver, for example, who is already engaged in running the shuttle, but despite that, she offers information with humor, when she could have just minded her own business. If everyone tried harder to exhibit this kind of behavior, it would make living on this planet so much more pleasant and easier.

I would like to say hello and shake the driver's hand as we leave the bus, but she's on a tight schedule and probably still has about twenty more rounds to go up and down the valley and lots of jokes to tell other passengers.

The day is not even half done, and M.'s plans involve lunch and wading in the Kanarra Falls.

We make a stop in Springdale at Blondie's Diner, a place frequently visited by M. in his many trips to Zion. Among the photographs and paintings of the valley, there are some funny boards hung on the deep purple walls of the restaurant, such as:

*"Charges for: - complaining 10¢, - whining 20¢, - pouting 25¢, - crying 50¢"*

*"The first five days after the weekend are always the hardest."*

*"Fly fishermen are born honest, but they get over it."*

*"Laugh and the entire world laughs with you, snore and you will sleep alone."*

M. recharges his batteries with an elk burger, and I indulge in mini tacos, mini corn dogs, and jalapeno cheese poppers, all deep-fried. Well, this has happened to me before. Apparently, I haven't learned from my mistakes. Out of natural curiosity, every time we eat out, I usually order something unfamiliar from the menu. Maybe three other times I managed to ask for fried food in different forms and consistencies. It is not that they aren't tasty, but after all the effort and heat suffered on the trails, fruits and vegetables would have been more nourishing. And elk burgers too!

In less than an hour, we reached Kanarraville, Utah, at mile 4,780, with our food digested and relatively rested for a new hike.

First, I have to explain how this place happened to be on M.'s list. Kanarraville is a little secluded town near St. George, Utah, an hour away from Zion National Park. In its vicinity, Kanarra Creek springs from the mountains through a beautiful slot canyon, creating several ravishing waterfalls that, up to one point, were a secret the locals kept for themselves–hence the name Southern Utah's Best-Kept Secret. Because of the popularity gained in social media, the place became increasingly trendy. The images captioned with a wrong #ZionNationalPark hashtag on Instagram has turned the five-mile trail to Kanarra Falls and back into a serious tourist attraction that the authorities of this little town of 350 people have had to deal with. When they noticed that each month more and more cars invaded their streets with no sign of decreasing, they took matters into their own hands. They arranged parking lots on the periphery of the town and overnight became owners of a natural park, which they learned how to manage and turn a profit. They started charging $10 per parked car and a $7 fee per person for visiting the waterfalls.

We park, we pay, and put on our water shoes, as most of the trail coincides with the creek. Dutifully, we follow the daily mantra: sunscreen applied on the face, shoulders, and arms, buffs iced in the cooler and fixed on heads, and a backpack filled with water bottles. Then, we are off to the trailhead.

It is a superb afternoon, but unbearably hot, at least until we find water, even if completely exposed to the desert sun. Every once in a while, we meet the winding brook that flows down to the village and cross it, getting wet up to our knees, splashing, and loudly fooling around. We traverse some steep inclines, where the water runs in miniature falls over glossy boulders, forming small natural pools, where kids wallow in peace. The closer we move from the canyon toward the exit of the creek, the vegetation thickens and the temperature cools. Finally!

From here on, we only walk through the water along the riverbank that has tall red stone walls instead of shores. The exotic feel of this place comes from two waterfalls running inside the canyon. You can climb them on rudimentary ladders (probably concocted by the locals excessively long ago, long before the tourists showed up).

At first sight, I say it is enough to have seen the first waterfall, as it is spectacular. I think to myself that climbing the next one shouldn't be a must. This is the voice of the coward in me, who is looking for effortless fun, but we are not even halfway through the vacation, and I don't think I can finish it on crutches. I am so lucky that M.'s voice is so much clearer and more convincing than my slightly old conscience. I proceed to climb both waterfalls without physical difficulties but with my heart throbbing in my throat.

I understand perfectly why someone would keep this oasis a secret, in the middle of the desert. I am also extremely happy to have spent an afternoon in its midst.

On our way back, we take photos with, on, under, and over the waterfalls, lurking around for the most opportune moment, when there are no other visitors around to ruin our shots and not to disturb the professionals who are trying to photograph the water with long-exposure.

Walking back to the car, I drag my feet through the water, intentionally splashing everywhere, and feel like screaming joyfully from the top of my lungs about this incredible day. I am so lucky!

Back in La Verkin, gray stifling smoke smears the sky to the north, proof of another wildfire. These fires seem to be natural all over the American West during the summer, but I am still not used to them. My heart aches whenever I think of the hundreds of square miles of devastated nature and all the wildlife that has to find shelter and food elsewhere. Although it has been clear to me, ever since Arizona, that fire matters in the forest's regeneration, the simple image of fire and unstoppable smoke convince me that, without them, the planet would be better off. So would be my sleep tonight. Sweet dreams.

# **14 -** *THE SUBWAY SLOT CANYON - ZION WILDERNESS, UT*

I t's July 4, 2018, and I am in the right place to celebrate Independence Day for the first time. I have great expectations and want to take part in all the festivities.

We leave the hotel at dawn, at the same time as a group of motorcyclists, the kind I have always seen in movies: black leather jackets, serious boots with thick soles, buckles and spikes, skull bandanas, tattoos, beards, and sideburns. There are maybe ten of them. I notice that a few are women. No beards or sideburns, obviously. There is something else unexpected for me. (I'm clueless bike-wise and only used to how things are in my country). Most of them are around sixty years old and seem to have been traveling this way ever since they were old enough to drive.

I watch them mount their bulky Harley Davidsons, equipped with stuffed leather saddlebags and tail bags, and I follow their every move as they prepare to leave. I wave to one of them as I step into the car, and he waves back with that American familiarity I so deeply appreciate.

Back home, motorcycles are proof of youth, virility, or rebellion against turning thirty, and under any circumstances is it a way of living. I have heard of gangs traveling together and riding inline on the national routes, but hardly ever have I seen such an image. This sounds like a story I heard in a bar.

Here, I see them everywhere, in groups of three or thirty, passing us on routes or interstates with that unmistakable roaring sound. M. tells me that this is what they do during the summer, scatter all over the West, especially to the national parks. To me, they are an exotic apparition and a manifestation of pure freedom of expression and movement. Considering that today is July 4, they look like an American symbol I get to study closely in the hotel parking lot in La Verkin, Utah.

Another American emblem is Subway (no, not the restaurant

chain that sells foot-long sandwiches), our destination for today. It is a second-time visit for M. and a first for me because of the incredible luck we had winning the lottery earlier this year. It being an extremely popular destination, the authorities had decided years ago to limit access to Subway, to preserve it. Now that I know what Subway is, I understand why they should limit the number of people going down there and that it might also have something to do with knowing how many come back at the end of the day.

Having been here before on different occasions, M. remembers the times when a permit was not necessary for visiting Subway. He tells me he always took the most difficult route, the one climbing down through a canyon descending directly into Subway. He is happy though to have won the lottery and to have the opportunity to revisit it today with me.

So, here we are on our way to one of the most emblematic places in the American West, the monumental spring of Left Fork North Creek through the Wildcat canyon walls, which towards the exit resembles a subway tunnel. There are two trails to get there. One is extremely challenging, and it involves the use of headlamps, harnesses, carabiners, and about 200 feet of rope for rappelling the canyon from the Wildcat Canyon Trailhead down to Subway, occasionally dropping in many of the creek's natural pools. It makes sense for M. to have chosen this trail and doing it while carrying a heavy load of mountain gear, as this is his kind of fun. The latter is only demanding. Therefore, we approach this one today.

My climbing abilities are relatively non-existent, and mainly this is why M. has to give up rappelling for walking this time to Subway, which cuts the fun in half for him. However, he would never admit it. I have a little hunch and start believing that his need for adventure will attract what is about to happen.

The trail entails hiking down from the Kolob Terrace Road to the Left Fork North Creek and then continuing against the stream to Subway. It is only nine miles. We hiked nine miles the other day, so I am not worried. I am most definitely able to make it to the subway tunnel, but what I do not yet know is that I will have to face many challenges to survive this festive day. Knowing M., I should have anticipated the hardship, but remembering all the difficulties I overcame with him by my side, I once again dive in trustingly and unconsciously. It can only be a fantastic experience!

It is 8 am, and we are in the parking lot on Kolob Terrace Road, where we park next to two other cars and one RV. While M. fills the backpack with water bottles, snacks, and water shoes, as most of the trail follows the creek, I go to the restroom. As I said before, there are not any glades used as public toilets, because the authorities kept in mind the basic human needs when creating the national parks, so every trailhead has an ecological restroom.

When I return to the car, I see M. talking to a man and a girl, hovering over a map and a GPS device. I say hello and then let them go back to their discussion. The two, father and daughter, had hiked the trail for fifteen minutes, and curiously enough, turned up back to the parking lot, not realizing they were walking in circles. The father, Mark, asks M. if he is familiar with the trail, and if so, could he and his daughter, Sydney, join us at least until the trail becomes more obvious so that they will not deviate again. Of course! M. was here before, although not necessarily from this direction.

*"Sure. It's easy and I know the way. It will be fine, don't worry. We'll go together."*

*"Oh, thank you, that's great! We're so lucky to run into you. It seems we wouldn't have seen The Subway today by ourselves."*

Sydney is the lucky person from their family who won the lottery, even though all the members had applied year after year with no success. The father is truly happy to share such an experience with his fourteen years old daughter. Certainly, this must be a memorable moment for a teenage girl to share with her dad. I too think we are so fortunate to be given this celebratory day, in a decor I already foresee as exotic, in the company of other people who had dreamt of coming here.

We walk one behind the other, with M. as our guide on this narrow sand trail. Among cacti and spiny desert shrubs. Every few steps, morning lizards cross our path with the speed of a thief chased by the police. We advance enthusiastically, more and more alert, while M. tells us in detail about his last visit here. He explains the exact order of how things should happen as he remembers them.

*"There should be a descent with switchbacks until we reach the valley, then walk against the stream, and then we should enter Subway. It's the same way back. Easy peasy lemon squeezy."*

Hmm. When we are talking mountains, desert, heat, and streams, the action rarely unravels as expected and there will be plenty of unexpected incidents. If M. finds it easy, that means it will be 99% more difficult for me. But these things don't cross my mind while the path is flat and unimpeded. Even if they would cross my mind at this point, I would still go on, just a little more aware of the situation I'm in by my own will. Only when M. starts descending, slender as a locust, down a field of small-car-size boulders, do I begin wondering if something might be off.

I ask if this is the right way, noticing there is not a trail per se, but hundreds of boulders randomly thrown by Sisyphus on a training day.

*"Yes, this is it. It's probably not as well maintained as I remember, but it gets us down to the river and, look, there are even some traces here and there,"* M. assures us.

*"Oh, that's good,"* says Mark, happy to be farther than he went on his first attempt.

It becomes clearer that we are not actually on a trail when every boulder we dismount is a little taller than I am, and we have to do it by sliding on our backs or bellies, while the one in front helps us jump and make sure we won't break any bones landing. I squint downward and try to see the river, but before my eyes there are only rocks stacked accidentally on top of each other. Hence, I presume I have nothing else to do but trust M. and hope that, at the end of this wild slope in Utah, there is indeed a creek and upstream the famous Subway. To be honest, all I want right now is to step onto a flat area and lose the fear that the boulders will crush me, like a peppercorn in a grinder.

I must admit. I go from whining in my head to doing it aloud, mainly because some rocks are not stable and I constantly imagine one of them rolling down and landing on someone's head, faster than we would scream *"Stones!"* I don't have a change of clothes and I am likely to stretch and unravel my leggings and catch my t-shirt on the abrasive surface of some rock.

Mark and Sydney are quiet, concentrating on safely shifting from one boulder to another, helping each other every step of the way. I know they too know we're not where we should be, but it's too late to mention it. Also pointless. They are just happy not to be alone on this adventure on July 4.

M. is more and more sprightly, going down in wide jumps with his long legs hardly touching the earth as if the boulders were giant soap bubbles he wouldn't want to break. He is way ahead of us, maybe 150 feet downhill, and his body language shows that he has good news. Getting closer to him, we can hear him say that we are indeed on the right trail as we too start hearing the creek's murmur.

A minute later, after my pulse slows down and my heart stops pounding in my ears, I do hear the water. I calm down imagining the coolness of the mountain at the end of the trenches. The thought of having to climb back up this entire rocky wall, assuming M. is right, and this is indeed the right trail, overwhelms me and makes it a bit hard for me to enjoy the experience.

After ten more layers of boulders, resembling huge coffee ice cream scoops clustered onto a too-small saucer, we reach the sandy riverbanks framed by the fragile green stalks of what seem to be willows. We find a shady place and take a well-deserved break, while the accumulated tension slowly dissolves into the sparkling, invigorating water.

Our new friends are from Oregon. He works in IT. She is a freshman in high school. Only the two of them are vacationing in the West, because his wife had left for Tokyo with her friends to celebrate a birthday. Then, we hike upstream in a line.

It is inexplicable how fast I can forget how hard it was to make it here, but at least I don't acknowledge it. What I do not forget is that it will be just as hard to climb back, but I simply refuse to make a priority out of this thought.

I look around and see a beautiful green wild gorge, unaltered by the humans, and from here, even the rough slope we climbed down with pain and sweat has a rare beauty. Tiny birds with restless flight and random rhyme songs ruffle the leaves of the trees and dive like experts into the clear shore. They then shake the water from their impermeable feathers with quick moves, too quick to discern.

We progress on the sand trail going parallel to the flowing water, every once in a while, having to push aside sagging nameless willow branches or going around chubby boulders, related to the ones from the descent. In places, the stream draws spontaneous curls, pushing the path over hunched tree trunks and leaves behind wet patches of land.

After approximately one mile, something that makes me yell, *"I told you so!"* greets us on the side of the trail, (I only scream it in my head, because I am alive and well, after all.) There, at the foot of the switchback, is the signage for the trail we hiked in parallel to. We are relieved that at least the return will be milder. Suddenly, the backpacks seem lighter, having escaped from climbing back up the boulder mountain.

Soon after this fortunate discovery, we meet a person that is definitely the same species as M., skipping and indifferent to high temperatures, long distances, and over 45° inclines. We greet each other enthusiastically and the young traveler assures us that Subway is worth it, although we still have a long way to go.

The side trails we have to take, to avoid the now abundant torrent of the stream, become narrower, and at some point, disappear into the steep walls of the gorge. A few times we cross the water by jumping from one rock to another, but we soon realize it would be easier just to walk right through the riverbank. Therefore, we put on our water shoes. Mark and Sydney don't have spare shoes, so they continue hiking through the water in their boots.

From now on, we walk like ducks through the creek that sometimes reaches up to our ankles and sometimes up to our knees. This is the ultimate treat in the desert heat. It is like having oversized ice cream instead of lunch. If you ever decide to visit Subway, bring a pair of water shoes, as they are light, the rubber sole is soft and prevents you from slipping, and the perforated fabric doesn't keep the water in.

As we walk up the river, the bank gradually changes its structure. The sand turns into rocks, then plump boulders, and then extensive areas of flat smooth stone covered with army-green, mustard-yellow, and brick red moss.

*"We're getting closer, guys!"* says M., who remembers this unusual-looking part of the trail.

The water drains on these wide, flat marble-colored stairs. Here and there, multiple waterfalls form where the stairs become narrow and craggy, flowing over frizzy bundles of moss. The chasm walls come closer and closer together and become more and more arched, like two parentheses, creating this impressive subway-like opening.

*"This is it! This is the famous Subway!"*

Even if I weren't aware this is what they call it, I would still think this place resembles a subway station. Nature's boundless imagination once more amazes me and I am so grateful to be its witness.

We cross the canyon until it narrows all the way and there is nowhere to go but up. We see a couple of climbers rappelling the vertical walls at the end of the tough trail. How lucky we are to see somebody getting to Subway the other way. We are mesmerized as we watch them climbing down the maybe thirty-foot-tall wall, hanging in harnesses on thick ropes, with heavy backpacks strapped to their backs, and descending into the natural pool the creek forms at the base of the walls. Applauses are in order while they get out of the ice-cold water, and we loudly express our admiration for the notable performance of the two.

Sydney and Mark take off their backpacks and start assembling the cameras and the tripods, each of them trying to find the best angle for capturing most of the beauty. Subway is one of the most photographed places in America. From what I have seen so far, I realize that mornings or afternoons would be the perfect timing to do so. It is midday, and the light enters perpendicularly into the canyon, creating black and white contrasts of light that ruin the pictures. We aren't that upset with this though, as the purpose of today was to find ourselves under the famous arches of the Wildcat Canyon. Which we do.

We take a brief break; eat lunch and then walk up and down, stopping at every pool that is inexplicably carved into the stone floor. M., like a restless foal, enters two pools up to his waist, laughing loudly and trembling with cold and adrenalin. I joined him in his gaiety.

We fill our eyes with the colors of this fantastic corner of the universe and our lungs with pure mountain air, then we say goodbye to our friends and head back. We want to reach La Verkin or St. George before nightfall to witness at least a bit of the Fourth of July festivities.

As usual, on the way back, I am more energetic. Maybe because I know what hardship to expect or maybe because I am loaded with the energy of the places I visit and disregard the hardness and fatigue of the trail.

On the way back, we wade more than walk, jumping in every natural pool we encounter and lingering under small waterfalls. Gray frogs leap all over, and a white one makes a stop on my hand while I lie on a stump stuck on the shore. I see a giant black-yellow butterfly resting in an orange flower and a dozen black and red dragonflies swarming around my fiery head. Then, for the first time in my life, I see a water snake. This is precisely when I decide to put my boots back on, leave the coolness of the water behind, and hit the sandy trail.

We laugh and point at every out of the ordinary thing we encounter, take photos, and from time to time make small talk with groups of people heading towards Subway.

After about two hours at a quick pace, we are getting closer to the intersection, with the switchback ascent that leads to the parking lot. My blood sugar is running low, and my hair is almost catching fire under the afternoon sun. I take the buff off my head and somehow place it on my shoulders, as I feel my skin peeling off, like plastic wrap. I remember Sydney having a safari hat, with wide brims and a T-shirt. As I am wearing a fitness tank top, I try in vain to cover myself with a too-short buff. Well, there is a lot to learn about hiking. It would not be a bad idea to buy myself a wide brim hat, but for now, I have to climb up the barren mountain, totally exposed to the desert sun.

I climb it with the last drop of strength I have and lots of sweat. I use the same technique from Zion: after every few switchbacks, I take a quick break to catch my breath. While I struggle up the incline and my calves tighten into two painful rocks, I remember the boulders I rolled down on in the morning and say thank you for having a not-so-less traveled path underneath my feet right now.

Everything hurts and all I want is to whine like a spoiled child, but I have no power to speak, just to act on it in my head. We passed a group of people we had met earlier in Subway, who were leaving as we reached there. They are now taking a break on the same narrow trail we are all climbing, obviously tired as hell. We say hello in sign language as they have no resources to articulate any words, and I am just as burned-out to reply.

But M., who seems as fresh as he was in the morning, full of contagious enthusiasm, stops for a moment to chat with them. I truly admire him for the way he carries his body up and down the mountains, as if he were weightless. I am so glad to see him in front of me, encouraging and assuring me I am just as capable. And, he is always right, despite all my laments.

After nine difficult miles under the Utah sun, we make it back to the car, turn on the air conditioning, take off our boots, peel off the socks from our feet along with at least one layer of skin, and put on our flip-flops. After every trail, we follow the same steps. Before we go, we think of our friends and hope they will make it back safely. We write them a note with our phone number, and email address and ask them to let us know they're OK and maybe exchange some photos. We leave the note in the driver's door of the RV and then go back to La Verkin.

We intend to head back to the hotel and freshen up for a night on the town. End the day on a celebratory note, American style. I truly am curious what it's like, especially after seeing so many movies where people cheerfully lie down on picnic blankets, watch the fireworks, drink beers, and eat hot-dogs. I would never say no to any of this, but all I have the energy for is shower and crash on the king-size hotel bed. I explain to M. that I have already celebrated July 4 in the most original way ever and that not even all the fireworks in the whole of Utah could make this day even more beautiful than it has already been.

Thank you, M.!

# 15 - *THE RED CLIFFS NATIONAL CONSERVATION AREA, SNOW CANYON STATE PARK, BRYCE CANYON, RUBY'S INN CAMPGROUND, UT*

At mile 4,850, we leave La Verkin greeted on both sides of the road by waving red, white, and blue flags. It's not too late to enjoy a bit of national celebration on our way to St. George, Utah. Hurricane and Harrisburg are just as festive. So is the serene sky that covers this desert, which, besides creating the most whimsical landmarks, also produces heat as a full-time job.

Because we are in the neighborhood, and M. is the man with a tight spreadsheet for everything worth visiting in the state of Utah, we make a stop in the outskirts of St. George's suburbs. The Red Cliffs National Conservation Area and the Snow Canyon State Park border the city to the North. We approach them one by one, but first, we park near the entrance toward the Paradise Canyon Loop Trail, which is literally across the street from a residential area.

As I step out of the car, I notice it is already so hot outside that I would be safer staying inside. I see a sixty+ women's group who have just finished hiking the trail. They are now loudly saying goodbye to one another and then head to their houses nearby. It looks like this is something they do regularly and will probably do it again tomorrow. I admit, watching old women embracing this kind of habit encourages me to follow their example. In my country, most of the women over sixty cook, clean, raise grandchildren, and for fun, they watch soap operas.

After the well-known procedure: sunscreen - water – wet buff, we cross the street and tackle the trail that covers most of the Red Cliffs National Conservation Area. The unbelievable blue sky above creates an unreal composition over the red landscape on this morning's canvas. The path goes smoothly up and down along phantasmal rocks, short or tall, chubby or pointy at the top. The elements perforated most of them, and they look like hundreds of birds have dug nests in their stone. Matte scale lizards, and long ear gray hares with white tiny scuts (obviously named cottontail rabbits), appear and disappear out of our vision like phantoms.

We are deep into the reservation when we meet another sixty + ladies' group and at least one of them looks to be eighty+, impeccably equipped with hiking shoes, pants, and trekking poles, all most likely bought from the REI's spring-summer collection. It was definitely a memorable feminine sight. One I would never see back home. Reaching a strong old age, with morning walks through the neighborhood state park, does not sound bad at all!

After passing the loop curl mid-trail, we encounter a group of teenagers riding mountain bikes that seem to practice a rather extreme sport, diving into the sand road, over rocks and boulders of different sizes and shapes at a speed that makes me close my eyes and cross my fingers for their safety.

We have been walking for just an hour, but we are already red and dehydrated like a couple of overcooked rotisserie chickens. We have almost finished the loop and can spot the car in the distance, dreaming of its AC system, but we choose to hang around a bit more. From up here, we can watch the city of St. George, the Virgin River that cuts it in two, baseball fields that add splashes of green to the red scenery, roads pointing uniform tentacles towards the suburbs, houses with turquoise pools and cacti gardens, and mountains stretched along the horizon.

Snow Canyon State Park is just a few miles away and the brochure we received at the entrance enumerates attractive trails like Butterfly Trail, Lava Flow Overlook, Petrified Dunes, Whiterocks Amphitheater, and Snow Canyon State Park Petroglyphs. We choose to visit Jenny's Canyon, another slot canyon we insist on seeing, it being a type we have not encountered so far. The only way I can describe it is a chocolate cake with several tiers from which you cut a thin slice (the cake is the mountain and the canyon is the space where the slice was cut). We enter the mountain through a wide opening, and as we go along, the walls get closer and closer to one another until they unite in an acute angle, and we can't go any further. It resembles a cave but a vertical one where you can see the sky until space and light retract.

We only saved this morning for exploring this corner of the world, and the rest of the day awaits us in Bryce Canyon National Park. To drive there, we have to cross the Zion Valley once more. This allows M. to say goodbye to his favorite park, and I can take a photo of the entrance sign I somehow missed four days ago. It is unacceptable not to have photos of all the totems from each park we visit.

Here we are, driving through Zion once more, west to east this time, greeted by tricolor flags hoisted on every lighting pole along the road and by thousands of tourists who animate the park into a joyful vacation bustle. We stop in front of the Zion totem that welcomes you on one side and wishes you farewell on the other. We take a few photos with the sign alone, the sign and me, and then with both of us with the help of a family that has stopped for the same reason. While waiting for them to take their place under the sign (so that we can return the photo favor), we notice about five big horn mountain sheep grazing pensively thirty feet from us. We take advantage of their proximity and goat-napped them from the landscape into our cameras and drive off to Bryce Canyon.

Utah is a treasure-state, where you can find a wonder of nature in any direction. It takes us less than an hour and a half to make it from Zion to a canyon that makes me exclaim, *"This can't be real!"* This is my first reaction when I lay my eyes on Bryce. My voice is several octaves above the norm, and I can't help but behave like a crazy person. I have already seen so many amazing places during this trip. Even so, my astonishment constantly climbs on the portative, until my exclamations sound like a raucous soprano. I never knew that the places M. has been showing me for the last two weeks even existed. Discovering them, I face an unforeseeable universe of boundless beauty.

At mile 5,003, we park at Ruby's Inn, a mountain resort that had turned a hundred in 2016. It is the major attraction in the Bryce area for accommodation and entertainment. It is the holiday village I don't want to leave. There is a general store, a buffet restaurant, RV and tent campground, teepees and cabins to rent, and outside pools and hot tubs. You can enjoy Bryce by only using your eyes and legs, a camera, and plenty of exclamation marks, but Ruby's elevates the recreation standard by offering you horseback riding, bicycles, ATVs, or helicopter rides. Our choice of movement through the canyons has always been classical, so this time we will count on our two lower limbs once more to move around.

First, we stop for lunch at Ruby's Inn Restaurant, and then at Sunset Point, where I see for the first time the spread of hoodoos[10] in the warm light of the afternoon. Here, I should leave a few empty lines… For a few minutes, I cannot make any sound at all. I just stand there in awe as tens of questions crush into one another in my shocked mind. Unfolding before my eyes are fifty-six sq. miles of canyon sprinkled with one-of-a-kind stone statues, despite being created in the same manner, and by the same culprits.

We hike down the Navajo Loop that joins the Sunset Point to the Sunrise Point. That carries us through the amphitheater of hoodoos giving us a chance to see these unearthly formations up close. I don't know if I should blame it on the sunset, but the landscape abounds in tones of beige, orange, mustard-yellow, and brick red.

Without having something to compare it to, I imagine I am walking with M. into an art gallery where nature exhibits its most eccentric sculptures. Most of them are nameless, but some stand out, resembling different worldly representations, with obvious names such as Thor's Hammer, Queen Victoria's Garden, Wall Street, and Two Bridges. It is amazing how water, wind, and a few tens of millions of years can transform stone into such unbelievable forms.

For the hoodoos to look like statues tens of feet tall, they first start by being just walls of stone. Then, after a few million years, they become windows, and then after another few million years, they can finally and proudly be called hoodoos.

Following the map, we stop at every important spot and try to match the name to the stone formations. It is like searching for clues while trying to find our way out of a maze we don't want to leave. The vegetation gets more and more abundant the deeper we walk into the canyon. The Zion Uinta chipmunks reveal themselves after the first switchbacks we hike down and they are extremely friendly. We spend a few good minutes watching them up close and they look as if they're posing for us. But really, they're just waiting for us to share a snack with them. We do them a solid and let them find their own food, helping them stay wild. We agree, M. and I, that Bryce, being so particular and unique, would deserve to have its very own chipmunks.

Although we have all morning tomorrow to wander again, it is hard for us to part ways with Sunrise Point, where the loop ends. However, we do it, after taking another dozen photos and staring over the ocean of hoodoos one more time. Then, we take over cabin No. 5 in Ruby's Inn Campground. Apart from the expected amenities of accommodation (picnic table, parking place, cabin with a porch and bench), we also have access to an outside pool and hot tub.

We end the day on a bubbly note, lazing about in a giant hot tub where we eavesdrop on a cool gang of middle-aged people. They talk about the fun they had today in Bryce and plan their next day. They reminisce about the good old days when they were in college and the vacations they used to take before they had kids. It's such a delight to witness how a group of people my age goes down memory lane, considering we experienced the same page of history in time, but in such different political and geographical circumstances, literally on the other side of the planet. Stepping out of the hot tub, we notice their tanned faces, necks, calves, and arms. Looking ridiculous. Just like us.

# 16 - *BRYCE CANYON NATIONAL PARK, ESCALANTE, CANYONS OF ESCALANTE RV PARK, UT*

In the early morning, we pack everything we unpacked last night with the dexterity and speed of a professional traveler. We leave the cabin keys in the drop-box the campground management placed at the exit for those of us leaving before 8 am. We found the same convenient box at every other campground on our journey.

We eat breakfast at Ruby's Inn Restaurant where, under very coincidental circumstances, the only grumpy people around are an older Romanian couple who were terribly upset that the buffet was not offering mashed potatoes. Not to mention that there must be at least fifty other dishes to choose from. What I want to point out is that their attitude in itself is un-American, I mean being discontent with what you have. The contrast between the couple and all the other sleepy customers on-site is striking. The simple fact of being in Bryce Canyon should cancel any negative culinary whim if you have eyes to look around and see where you are.

We are stuffed with bacon (Have I told you already how delicious bacon is in America?), and this is a sign of an amazing morning. We sit up less gracefully than usual. Personally, I hope the bacon will give me enough energy to face the eight-mile hike we are about to start. Just to feel safe, I stuff a bag of beef jerky into the backpack before we go.

Fairyland Loop Trail descends deep into the middle of the canyon and then follows a wide loop on its rim, arriving back at the beginning of the trail after eight miles. It is around 8 am, and there aren't any other tourists with whom to share the trail. Miles on end, it is just us two, spoiled by the splendid morning light and silence that the depth of the earth seems to exhale. We only cross paths with a few couples and small groups on the other side of the loop.

We hike up and down along millions of years of geological

architecture, with eyes wide-open and dropped jaws, noticing from up close the random shapes of hoodoos. Some are massive and compact like cruise ships, others isolated and thin like candles on a birthday cake. Some make you think of monks praying under their hooded robes, and the most inexplicable ones resemble window frames through which the image of the canyon reproduces itself for as far as you can see. The names are a great help to the imagination: Tower Bridge, Boat Mesa, Sinking Ship, and Crescent Castle.

The climax of the trail takes place at Paria Point, close to where we started the morning walk. This is where we witness, fully unprepared, a scene that seems to be inspired by a classic horror movie or a circus gig. We see a girl bite into a slice of bread, and then a black crow snatches it from her mouth in full flight. Hmm. Neither us, nor the blue tuft bird on the pine tree next to the bench where we are sitting, nor the chipmunks lined up on the fence in front of us, can express anything other than bewilderment. It is, however, a memorable moment, but that's about it.

It's almost noon, and my bacon-fueled energy is now depleted. But, not for M. He is just as energetic as he was a few hours ago, although I can assure you, he did not eat more bacon than I did. Therefore, he makes this subtle comment about peeling me off the bench, on which I collapsed maybe twenty minutes ago and suggests we head off to Escalante, where lunch awaits us. That was all I needed to hear to put myself in motion, that one of the main meals of the day is calling my name. I sit up and sprint the last mile back to the car.

At mile 5,107, we park in front of a restaurant in the so-called Escalante town. Well, it looks like Escalante Street rather than an urban settlement. Although it's an exclusive tourist area, it looks deserted. But summertime is not considered the peak season around here. Apart from two other restaurants, a gas station, a mini-market, a few houses, and the Grand Staircase Escalante National Monument Visitor Center, all you can see in every direction is an orange desert dotted with strange rock formations poking the horizon.

I am not used to arriving at a national park and not finding hundreds of visitors busy planning hikes and taking photos. Even in the restaurant, there are less than ten people including the cook, the waiter and us.

M. knows why we're here and what we have planned for the next few days. His explanations, referring to names such as Devil's Garden and Goblin's Lair, and his expert hiker enthusiasm, don't enlighten me about why we are the only people in this spot on the map. Here is why. Unlike the other parks we have visited, which had become national monuments protected by law a hundred years ago, Grand Staircase Escalante is one of the last places in the United States to be mapped. It was declared a national park during Bill Clinton's administration, back in 1996.

There is still a lot to learn about this area, and so geologists, explorers, and scientists build their careers in places like this. What has been already discovered, marked, and named are unique spots because of their wildness and difficult access that attract only a certain type of tourists, like M. (who knows he can handle it), and me (who trusts in M.).

There aren't any hotels around, but there is Canyons of Escalante RV Park where we have booked cabin No. 3. The campground offers five cabins for a maximum of four people each, twenty-five spots for RVs, and six for tents. At first glance, we only see a few people in the shade of an RV awning and just one tent. It looks pretty desolate in the bright afternoon light but clean and colorful because of the yellow and purple flower bushes scattered all around the place.

We settle in and then relax on the porch while attending to our intellectual interests. I read *Wild* and from time to time, I look at the barren mountains in the distance. M. studies the maps we will need in the morning and shares with me details about the trails. Once again, I trust him and my survival abilities. Therefore, I ignore the number of miles he tells me about and the elevation levels, especially since the destinations have such childish names like Peek-A-Boo Canyon and Spooky Gulch.

# 17 - *GRAND STAIRCASE-ESCALANTE NATIONAL MONUMENT, DRY FORK SLOT CANYON, PEEK-A-BOO CANYON, SPOOKY GULCH, DEVIL'S GARDEN, TORREY, UT*

At sun-up, we have breakfast at the picnic table in front of the cabin - salad, tomatoes, bell peppers, cheese, and canned tuna. The usual for a camp day. The heat has not launched yet, like a net over the land, so the air is bearable and doesn't chase us indoors. Across from us, we notice three more tents set up since last night. The neighborhood grew more animated, but it makes no difference to us, as we won't be coming back here tonight.

On the hiking websites, they describe Peek-a-boo Canyon and Spooky Gulch as the perfect choice for families with children, where they can enjoy a pleasant walk or play hide and seek. Consequently, my expectations for July 7, 2018, involve a fun trail into a childish yet unusual landscape.

We have to drive thirty miles, which would normally take us twenty minutes, but the roads in Grand Staircase Escalante are not all paved yet. It takes us an hour and a half to check in at this improvised parking lot. When I say improvised, I mean there is another car parked where the road we're coming from intersects with another road that looks like only off-road vehicles should use it.

We put our car to the test while visiting White Pocket. This time we decide to keep it safe by letting it wait for us, parked in the middle of the desert. Then, we walked the dirt road aligned with cacti, short juniper trees, and thistle shrubs. After a mile and a half, we reach the trailhead where this loud group of people of all ages is taking a photo and chanting joyful and encouraging words. Once again, I am certain that what is about to happen is just child's play.

We leave the group behind and start a mild descent, hopping from one flat rock to another, towards a wide valley entirely uncovered, vulnerable under the morning sun. There aren't any trail signs along the way, just cairns left behind by other travelers. At the bottom of the natural stairs, we find the first sign guiding us to the Dry Fork Slot Canyon, on a sand path bordered by sandy miniature bushes. The area is highly populated with big, glossy, green lizards and other small, matte, gray ones.

The trail that takes us to today's destinations first goes through Dry Fork, a broad canyon with tall rock faces that abound in coolness. Soon after we leave it, the fun begins. Yet it is a different kind of fun than what I had in mind.

We must approach the two canyons from a specific direction, M. explains to me. West to east, starting with Peek-a-boo and ending with Spooky because of reasons yet unknown to us. We follow the directions precisely and for a while walk along a tall crag. Then, we reach the entrance to Peek-a-Boo Slot Canyon, which isn't exactly accessible to kids. Nor to me, to be honest.

To enter the canyon, I have to climb a ten-foot tall polished and slippery boulder, with no evident stone holds. I am not one to free climb and my bouldering skills are nonexistent. Even if I had them, I would still not be able to climb this rock, as it is overhung. This is the first peek-a-boo I stumbled upon today and I fear for the parents from the cheerful group coming behind us who will have to deal with it as well.

Don't forget that I am with M. in this rocky paradise, and while I have a sip of water and scratch my head asking myself how could today turn out great after all, M. has already planned the following steps:

*"This is what we do: I squat and you climb on my shoulders first. I sit up and lift you, and then you can climb the rock on your own much easier."*

I do not know why I worried, really, even for a minute. I do exactly as I'm told. I climb on his shoulders, which I will probably mark with the shape of the soles of my shoes, as I don't exactly have the weight of a ballerina. He sits up, and I pull myself on the rock, grabbing any stone bump I can find and slip into the canyon. M. throws me the backpack, and in about two and a half moves, he's in, next to me, using a method I cannot reproduce, but which I applaud intensely, happy to be together in the canyon.

Indeed, once we're in, peek-a-boo is exactly what we feel like doing, as the walls are relatively tight and contorted, with all kinds of polished stone hideouts and hollows of different sizes and creative shapes. Now and then, M. has to push or pull me when the canyon gets too steep. In places, I just slide on my belly or my back or jump from reasonable heights, and mostly just have a lot of fun. The exit is not as spectacular, because the canyon widens a bit giving way to a sand trail that leads us out into the desert.

Very close by is the entrance into the Spooky Gulch which comes with its own set of challenges for me. This time it is an elongated slot through some overhung boulders, narrow at the top and wider toward the bottom. The waters of an unstoppable storm seem to have thrown these rocks one on top of the other millions of years ago.

I don't have the exact facts, but as I assess the situation, nothing is to my advantage. Let's say I can somehow squeeze through, but then I would have to jump ten feet down to get inside. To M., things are simple as usual. While I complain quietly, he props his long stork legs against the opposing rocks, leaning on his hands, and then leaps like a gymnast onto the sand below, landing safely on his feet. Then he tells me:

*"This is what we do: Push your back to the right stone and your hands to the left one. Then, slide down bit by bit until you reach my shoulders with your feet. Keep your balance with your palms against the opposing walls as I bend down, and when you think you are low enough, jump!"*

Hmm. I understand perfectly what M. is telling me. At least theoretically. It seems to be a simple tactic with a successful outcome. As I try it and follow the steps, I have the distinct feeling that I will break either my head or some of my limbs in the fall.

Another couple shows up behind me, and their presence adds another layer of pressure on me, making me lose the bit of focus I have gathered so far. Smiling, I ask them to be patient because it will be a while until I will climb down. They take a few steps back, giving me enough space. So, I bravely approach the multiple obstacle vertical displacement.

I try again the way M. suggests, but I am too afraid. I lie on my belly and slide easily until I feel my feet on M.'s palms, but I don't dare detach myself from the cliff for fear I will break his arms. I try sliding on my back with my legs apart into an unfortunate split, leaning on my elbows. But this takes me nowhere. I turn on all sides; try another split followed by a front-flip and a cartwheel to the amusement of the couple. Then, tired of my fear and absurd poses, I just let go and slide on my back. M. catches my feet in his palms, grabs my knees, then my thighs, and finally I jump as my heart gets stuck in my throat.

Unlike M.'s elegant leap, I land on all fours, looking ridiculous and thanking gravity for not causing me lifelong damages. I can't tell for sure, but I think the couple applauded me, probably for climbing down this portion in less than fifteen minutes, which took M. less than a minute. Anyway, I am here, in the canyon, whole, unharmed and thankful. M. goes:

*"See? Piece of cake! You did great!"*

I try to contradict him, but realize it would be in vain and besides, he is right. One way or another, I did manage to descend, mostly like Alice down the rabbit hole, but you know what? I am proud of myself! And so, I continue the hike through the suspiciously dark slot canyon, thinking to myself that the worst is now over. Behind us, the other two climb down in maybe three minutes, but I will not let someone else's performances discourage me.

The decor is similar to the first canyon, except the walls are arched, uneven, and grained. There is less light inside, and as we advance, I understand why it is called Spooky. There is not enough room for fooling around here, no place to hide, sit or bend. The path is wider than a swimmer's shoulders and at some point, we can only move laterally.

The walls are so close together that I have to stand with my feet in the ballet first position (the one with the heels held together and the toes pointed in opposite directions). Sometimes

I have to bend forward or backward following the shape of the space between the walls and it gets spooky when my body has the exact dimension of that space. If my chest or hips were even a few inches bigger in girth, I could not move ahead.

Strong feelings of elation and adrenalin mix in my mind, in effervescent cocktails that make me shout out of both delight to live this unique experience and terror that I might not be able to squeeze through. Or worse, to be stuck and have to bring people to blow up the mountain to remove me from here. It's not ideal for me to shout (really, maybe just in my mind), because if I would breathe in enough air for a scream, then the walls would for sure trap me in.

For about thirty minutes, I live in a foreign film, playing the character of a fearless heroine that descends into the depths of the earth following her lover's example. I see M. advancing in front of me, constantly checking my progress. I am so pumped that I could jump around, giggle and hug M. to express my state of mind, but I have to take up as little space as possible, so I settle for blowing him a kiss.

Somewhere toward the end of the canyon, we cross paths with a couple that wasn't aware they had approached the trail backwards. Lucky for them, the path has widened and we can pass them with little difficulty. I wish I were a tiny nimble lizard, to sneak back into the canyon and see how the couple will pass the other couple coming behind us. They will certainly have to walk back to a wider area to let the others pass. But what happens if there are even more people coming this way? Well, this is a funny perspective to a potentially crowded situation, unless this couple will make it to the other end of Spooky Gulch. I seriously doubt they will be able to climb up from where we had to jump. Anyway, everybody has their challenges to face, so we mind our own business and head back to the car.

On our way back, in the same spot where we met the loud group this morning, we meet a disoriented couple. We say hello, as usual, and then the man approaches M. and asks him for directions, as there were no signs to follow. We find out that they want to hike the same trail that we hiked, without having down-loaded the maps from Google Maps. This makes us realize these people don't know what they are getting themselves into. But this is the least of their problems. Even if they somehow reach the trailhead, they do not stand a chance of going through, as the man is approximately twice as heavy as M. and the woman is at least fifty pounds chubbier than I am. As I said before, I was fill-ing up the available space in the gulch with my size.

We explain to them the conditions of the trail and try to imply, as delicately as possible, that they will not fit inside. It is an indelicate job telling someone they are too large to do some-thing, and it feels so wrong. We don't know if we made ourselves clear or if we were indeed too subtle, because after we leave, they remain pensive for quite some time on top of that mesa. I hope they ended up making the better choice.

After approximately seven miles and a few hours, we are back to the improvised parking lot, which is now busier with new cars and a white van packed with Asian people. We take off our boots, put on flip-flops, and eat something in the shade of the trunk door. When we're about to hit the road, the driver of the van asks us in broken English if it's OK for them to drive the van up to the trailhead. M., in very explicit and categorical English, advises him NOT to do such a thing. Firstly, because only 4x4 vehicles can ride the dirt road, and secondly because the trail requires hiking apparel and experience. He emphasizes the last part because all the people in the van are dressed in black slacks and white button-up shirts, dresses, and flats. We don't want to be critical and unfair, but we also would rather not have to alert all the rangers in the park to come and rescue the group lost in Grand Staircase Escalante.

We return to Escalante under an ink-blue sky, interrupted here and there by fluffy white clouds. It looks like it's only sunny in this area, on a few-mile radius. Farther away in the direction we are driving the sky is opaque, overcast, and heavy. We have been on the road for seventeen days now, and it only rained when we left Illinois and watched the pouring water through the car's sunroof. Ever since then I've already forgotten what rain clouds look like and now, we are about to witness a desert storm.

In the distance, above Escalante, the clouds break and we can see the downpour over the rocky expanse. With the risk of being caught in the rain, we have one more stop before returning to town.

On the other side of the canyons, there is Devil's Garden (abbreviated) or Devil's Garden Outstanding Natural Area within the National Landscape Conservation System (unabbreviated). It is a rather limited area where hoodoos of diverse shapes stand scattered randomly. It took the weather only 166 million years to create an unlikely garden that was declared a world heritage site exactly the year I was born. That is 1979.

It is still sunny when we arrive there and we are lucky enough to explore the garden without being rushed by calamities. These hoodoos differ from the ones in Bryce Canyon, and they make me think of the *Sphinx* and the *Babele*[11] in the Bucegi Mountains of Romania. Yes, different shapes and sizes of sphinxes and grannies sprinkled all over. Wherever I look, I see cliffs with human or animal profiles. In particular, two elephants attract my attention, because they seem to join their trunks forming a delicate bridge.

Some of them are thick at the base and get thinner towards the top, others vice versa, somehow ignoring the laws of physics. Regardless of their looks, extraterrestrial forces seem to have placed them here as if for an art project.

I notice that many of the names of tourist destinations refer to devils, evils, and deaths. At least so far, we have seen the Devil's Bridge, the Devil's Elbow, and the Devil's Garden, none of them resembling anything frightening. A lot more places with bleak names and divine appearances await us from now on, and someday we will discover the meaning behind the names.

Whatever they call this place, we cannot overlook it. Especially since we are in the neighborhood. This place adds to the long list of natural monuments, which seem to have no explanation for their existence, despite all the information, the factors and processes that contributed to them looking the way they do.

We leave the Devil's Garden fascinating site, with adrenalin still pulsing in my veins ever since Spooky Gulch, when we find ourselves brushed by a sand tornado, long before entering the furious storm that has landed over Escalante. I have this sensation of coolness, after being haunted by the desert sun for hundreds of miles from Texas to Utah. I feel my skin hydrating just by looking at the water splashing against the windshield. This must be the first rain in months, and the desert will accumulate enough water for the plants and animals to last them as long as possible. This looks like a blessing. Pure joy.

We stop for lunch at Boots Café, where we have burgers with buns branded with the shape of a boot, and of course, a small mountain of fries. Apart from us in the restaurant, there is a French family and a group of local teenagers, dressed in jeans, cowboy hats, and boots with spur straps. All of us, including the servers, pray that the rain will not stop soon. We eat quietly, eyes glued to the windows.

The rain is still in full fling over Escalante when we leave for Capitol Reef National Park. Just a few miles down the road, the pavement is dry. The rain remains only in the rearview mirror, disrupting the horizon. We have seventy more miles to go, but we are in no hurry. We have to cross Boulder Mountain at an elevation of 10,000 ft.

Soon, the scenery gets greener and the road more and more winding with mountain curves. We entered a beautiful pine and birch tree forest. Now and again, we have to stop and let deer and herds of cows with no shepherd pass. We take a break on top of the mountain and take photos of the sign reading 9,600 feet. It's the highest altitude I have been so far. A personal record, although I reached driving. Not climbing.

We land in Capitol Reef National Park at mile 5,235 and take a short walk, just to take in the view, and admire the symbol of the park: the Chimney Rock. I think it doesn't look like a fireplace, but rather like an oversized terracotta stove, capable of heating a fifty-mile radius with just the heat it accumulates during the day. Regardless of its resemblance, it is a colossal sight, visible from Utah State Route 24. Since we are here and it is still daylight, we hike down to Panorama Point and Goosenecks Overlook, a stretch of red stone and short mountains of pastry and caramel cream.

The landscape, although related to every piece of Utah we have seen so far, stands out. Driving deeper into the park on our way to the hotel, every few miles the picture keeps its shape but fades its color. From the dark red of the Chimney Rock, the mountains fade into light orange, then light yellow, and then light blue. By the time we reach the hotel, they look like layers of sponge cake with pistachio and mint curd.

Sleep finds us tonight in room 208 at the Rodeway Inn, looking out the window at the pastel mountains.

# 18 - *CAPITOL REEF NATIONAL PARK, GOBLIN VALLEY STATE PARK, MOAB VALLEY RV RESORT AND CAMPGROUND, UT*

T he next day we wake up ambitiously early to have breakfast at the hotel, however continental it might be, because the managers are not even awake yet. There is nothing else around, except the mountains and the highway, so our only hope for a bagel with cream cheese and omelet is compromised. Still, we insist on ringing the doorbell at reception, at least to drop the key if not for breakfast. Finally, a fifty-something woman with long, tousled hair, still in her pajamas, opens the door with a big smile and lets us in.

*"Early birds beat the heat,"* says the woman with an appreciative attitude towards us, seeing that we are all geared up for a hike.

Then, her husband shows up, just as wrinkled and amiable. The two have been managing the Rodeway Inn Hotel together for a few years now, and this is where they live, permanently. They tell us about the busy times during the summer, something we are familiar with, and about the best time to visit the area, which is February-March. That is when they love to hike the mountains, when there are just a few others on the trails and the hotel is quite empty.

We have all morning to discover a concentrated percentage of the immense park, which would normally take us more than a week to visit completely. We choose trails to two spectacular destinations, both of them entailing natural stone arches sculpted by wind and water in a grandiose manner.

To get to Cassidy Arch, our first choice, we climb a tiramisu mountain, dusted abundantly with cocoa powder. We walk up and down countless ladyfingers soaked in coffee, cross paths with several wild turkeys, and after a few dozen switchbacks, Cassidy appears before us in all its stone glory. It is curvy and wide, like the agape mouth of a prehistoric cave.

This is where the Cassidy Arch Canyon Trail begins, an extremely popular route among the climbers. The arch we steal in our photos is, in fact, where they first rappel from, about 150 feet down. It is followed by another five similar rappels in total. I am happy just watching this eccentric manifestation of nature from the outside, but I can tell M.'s mind is currently imagining complex moves involving a harness, rope, and other trinkets with names known only by the likes of him. I suggest he comes back one day to make up for this too prudent summer, but he tells me not to worry and that he has already rappelled as much as to last him for at least ten more years.

The next stop is Hickman Natural Bridge, a massive stone structure that maintains its bridge shape against all laws of physics. The opening between the two pillars is at least 160 feet wide, and the scenery that penetrates in both directions is my favorite for the day.

Trekking up to it we follow a family with two children, a boy and a girl, both teenagers, both impatient for this hike to be over. And two parents much too patient for the situation at hand—heat, sand, and two successors way too ungrateful for this western vacation. The father keeps trying to offer bits about the Hickman Bridge and Capitol Reef, but the two kids keep on mocking him and would rather he left them alone. I, on the other hand, find the whole thing an effortless learning opportunity and ask the father to read louder from the brochure, as I am curious to find out as much as possible about this place.

Thus, I enjoy having a personal guide for this trail, from whom I learn that although this is not a volcanic area, petrified black lava stones are scattered all over the park.

With Capitol Reef behind us, we head northeast, to Goblin Valley State Park, Utah. An hour away. M. has been dreaming of rappelling into the Goblin's Lair for more than half a year. Trust me, it only sounds playful and makes you think of a little elf hut. In reality, I discover soon enough that the word *playful* is in total opposition to the grotto in question.

For now, I am enthusiastic about visiting this valley of goblins. I'll get to watch M. elegantly descend sixty-five feet into the lair. This is the only rappel he wants to do on this trip. He is aware though that I can't accompany him, so he would rather do everything together. Although the harness and rope are in the trunk, he decides at the last moment to only hike the trail and look at the cave from above.

We step out of the car into a crushing heat and notice that most of the tourists are ending their visits and heading to their cars. I don't feel like hiking anymore, for fear I might evaporate in the meantime. But, I too want to do everything with M. So, we start the three-mile trail that soon feels like thirty.

What we have to do is walk a mile and a half, to where the goblin in question has his hiding place, and then a mile and a half back through the exposed desert. We do just that until we arrive at a mountain of piled up boulders, climb up the scree, and there it is, the entrance to the lair. M. descends into it like a weightless chipmunk, jumping from one rock to another for about sixty feet down, and then shrieks with joy and asks me to join him:

*"C'mon, Raluca, get down here,"* he says, truly believing I shouldn't miss this.

*"Not me. I'll be right here, watching and waiting for you to come back up,"* I reply after I find a safe rock to sit on in the shade.

Even if I would climb down by a miracle, it is quite clear I couldn't climb back up. And the rope is in the car's trunk. I don't want to spoil M.'s joy with speleology interventions, so I wait patiently in this tiny shady spot, already dreading the way back.

I am even more nervous than the two teenagers from Capitol Reef, mostly because the only way we can return to the car is by walking through this heated stove. For the first time, I am terrified. We are alone in the middle of the desert. It is infernally fiery. I would take a break, but there is no hiding from the sun. I feel my hot breath when I exhale, and I expect my hair and buff to catch on fire at any minute, although I constantly wet it. I am certain that if I stayed over ten seconds in the same place, the soles of my boots would melt and glue to the rocks. M. keeps telling me it will be fine, that there's nothing to worry about. However, I am so ashamed to admit how afraid I am, thinking at any moment the gigantic birds circling above us in the sky will probably eat us.

As usual, M. is right. We return safely to the parking lot with just my fears bubbling all over the place. I calm down as soon as I find myself under the roof of the vista point shelter, and then I ponder the incredible endurance one can muster when there is no other way out. Well, I could have thrown a tantrum, cried like a baby, and asked for a helicopter to come to extract me from that furnace, but honestly, that would have been much more tiring than just walking.

So here I am, once again saved by my hidden resources and M.'s endless trust in me. Spiritually, M. is the one making me face my worth through these experiences and gives me the priceless gift of finding out what I am made of.

I sit on a bench at the edge of a large roofed picnic area, facing the Goblin Valley. I drink a Mike's Hard Lemonade and watch M. walking around, taking photos of the dwarf hoodoos resembling thousands of stone goblins. What turned this place into a protected natural area is the six square mile stretch of desert randomly covered by rock formations similar to the ones in Bryce Canyon. Only a lot shorter.

Goblin Valley and Bryce are the widest hoodoo-covered areas in the world. Here, they look like hunched little creatures with wool hats stuffed on their heads. Others say they look like mushrooms. The more I watch this valley, the more it looks to me like a bowl of chocolate caramel popcorn. Maybe I'm just starving.

Thinking of lunch (or rather dinner), we head to Moab, where we will spend the next two nights in one of the campgrounds. Halfway there, we exit the interstate and take a break in Green River, a small town with less than a thousand residents but with at least one Mexican restaurant according to Google Maps.

La Veracruzana Restaurant is empty, probably because we popped in here right when the lunchtime was over, as we usually do after a long morning out. At least we are served right away, and, considering the level of our hunger, this alone deserves ****, as many as the restaurant has on TripAdvisor. If you ever visit this restaurant, and can't decide what to have, I recommend bacon-wrapped shrimp with rice and beans. This is certainly a dish you won't find back home. The portions are so big that we have to take most of them to-go and eat them for dinner.

At mile 5,474, we land in Moab, a tourist city with the same attributes as Kanab, a destination for everyone who wants to visit Canyonlands and Arches National Parks. We first stop by a supermarket to stock up on food and water to last us for two days. As I get out of the car, I have the distinct desire to stay in and not get out. I don't know how to deal with the extreme desert heat and broiling asphalt combined with the atmosphere. It forces me to sprint inside the air-conditioned store as fast as my flip-flops allow me.

We have reservations in Moab Valley RV Resort and Campground, somewhere in the outskirts of town, at the bottom of some chocolate mountains where zip lining is very popular. The evening is not as stifling as it becomes overcast and should rain any minute. But, we are not so lucky as to live through rain twice in the same week.

Speaking of the week, I realize that ever since we left Illinois, I haven't been aware of which day of the week it is at any given moment. I don't know what day of the week it is today. It's just fascinating how the mind does not hold on to useless information when there is no pressure.

The wind is about to tip something over, anything really, that's how strong it is, but the air it blows through the campground is warm and thick.

The cabin No. 23 that accommodates us for two nights is just as nice and comfortable as the one in Escalante, but the campground is maybe five times bigger. And it seems to be fully booked. Across from us, there is a recreation area with picnic tables, a playground, and life-size chess and backgammon boards, with all pieces ready for battle. As I don't know how to play either of them, I politely refuse the games and read a little before going to sleep.

# 19 - *CANYONLANDS NATIONAL PARK, DEAD HORSE POINT STATE PARK, UT*

On our list for today, we have Canyonlands National Park and Dead Horse Point State Park. The latter lies inside Canyonlands like a state within a state, just like the Vatican and Italy.

The morning is ours before it is anybody else's. We cut the vegetables into big chunks and stuff them, along with the other ingredients we find in the cooler, into some very small bowls. Then, we cover everything in ranch dressing. This, once again, is the classic campground breakfast.

Canyonlands National Park is not only the set of the renowned *Thelma & Louise* movie but also an orgy of canyons, mesas, buttes, and arches dug by the Colorado River, Green River, and their tributaries in Southeast Utah. It covers over 500 square miles of the Colorado Plateau.

There are three areas to this park: Island in the Sky, The Needles, and The Maze. We cover the entire park and stop at every vista where the landscape duplicates the Grand Canyon again and again in shorter and wider shapes, scattered in places with sun burnt hoodoos, watered by rivers of green.

First, we choose a trail that gets us on top of the plateau from where we can admire and comprehend its extravagant vastness. We hike up to Mesa Arch, an archway of orange stone that frames this mesmerizing landscape of Navajo sandstone mountains, the secret language calligraphy of the canyon valleys, and the light blue tones of the horizon. We are in love with these arches and impressed with their unlikely becoming, mostly because the scenery resembles a painting in the oversized art gallery of Nature.

The second trail takes us to False Kiva, an unmaintained path in Island in The Sky, where the ancient Pueblo people left a small token of their legacy, an archeological site built using the sacred geometry[12]. Close to the top of the mesa, in a deep overhang, we

141

find the ruins of a grave or a praying spot in the shape of a perfect circle made of stones, maybe fifteen feet in diameter. Having an extremely fragile structure, the site is closed to the public and can only be observed from a certain distance.

Looks like the park hides several such ruins, but to preserve them as best as possible and not endanger their frail nature, the park brochure does not mention them and the trails are not maintained. If asked, the rangers offer information about the whereabouts of these sacred ruins, but otherwise, only those who search on purpose can find them.

We search for a picnic area where we can put together a quick lunch from the contents of our cooler. By sheer accident, we found the perfect place with a free show. One would think that the rain we left behind in Escalante made its way here somehow, because on the flat rock in front of us, there are tiny pools formed in round shallow hollows.

We're eating in silence, admiring the scene, when a chipmunk, with a severe case of ADHD, shows up out of nowhere, running as if controlled by a remote control from one pool to the other. It dips its nose in the little puddle and water drops drain from its whiskers onto its brown striped fur. It then stands on its rear paws and seems to have smelled our lunch, because it gets closer to us with widened nostrils and a funny trembling nose. As soon as it stepped into the shade under the picnic area's roof, it comically fell down on its belly, with its four paws stretched out. We imagine it making sounds of pleasure caused by the stone's coolness. It waits for a few seconds, skeptically, maybe we will give in and offer it something to eat, and then it's on its way.

It is now time to pay a visit to the Dead Horse Point State Park, which is a 6,000-foot altitude mesa, from where you can enjoy watching the green flow of the Colorado River and the spectacular curl it makes, much like the Horseshoe Bend.

This area became a distinct park because of the unrestricted visibility of the river and the canyons, but the name comes from a rather bleak legend. Talk about the western attractions named after Dead, Death, or Devil. The list goes on.

They say that before the 1900s, herds of wild mustangs used to live in the area. The cowboys would herd and force them to climb this very mesa, blocking their exit with an enclosure. They would harness the horses and try to break them. Then, they would only leave a very narrow gate open through which they could find their way back down into the canyon. The horses that discovered the gate would be sold at fairs. The ones that weren't smart enough, and therefore didn't find their way out, were abandoned on this terrace. They would soon die of thirst, watching the Colorado River from the steep rim. I find this to be a very cruel way of selecting the pureblood horses. Although effective.

I fall asleep thinking of the wild mustangs, the pueblo people, and their similar stories and destinies in which the white man had such a strong role.

# 20 - *ARCHES NATIONAL PARK, BEAVER, UT*

A rches National Park is our last destination before heading west and getting a bit closer to the Pacific Ocean. Because we intend to hike more trails than yesterday, and then drive to Beaver, Utah, we wake up even earlier than usual. The sun is still in its pajamas, head on the pillow, and sound asleep.

We leave the campground before dawn and arrive at the park entrance when the horizon is shyly reddening, unveiling the ghostly shapes of the cliffs. There are groups of people bordering the side of the road that seem to have come on purpose this early to catch the sunrise. We park the car and do the same. We don't yet understand why they were here precisely, but we get it as the sun is about to rise.

We're all sitting on the curbside with our cameras in pole position. We loudly express our amazement at each inch of light the sun is casting over the horizon, as the lenses try to focus on the beam of light in the still dark landscape. The sun casts its first ray between the fantastic cliffs in the distance, then a second stronger one. In about two minutes, the entire miracle of the sun rising concentrates in one spot over the vast desert. With my eyes focused on the light and my peripheral gaze stretched out wide, I print in my mind one of the most spectacular pictures from the Wild West.

When the sun loses its color and enhances its army of lumens, we leave it to do its job and head to the Devil's Garden trailhead, where we are among the first to arrive in the parking lot. We chose the longest trail, because it will take us near the largest number of impressive stone arches in the park. Actually, on the planet.

Arches National Park gained its name because of the 2,000 plus arches that reside on its one hundred square miles-territory, which also makes it one-of-a-kind in the entire world. Except for these arches, across the park there are a series of stone formations that compete in beauty with the ones from Monument Valley and Capitol Reef.

As we left the cabin before the break of dawn, we didn't have time to eat breakfast; we stuffed the bowls with leftovers and started munching, sitting on the curbside. Meanwhile, across the street from us, a couple is busy extracting the entire contents of their car through the wide-open doors. The sight of them and all their possessions on the sidewalk intrigues us, and the whole scene becomes entertaining when the man approaches us. He says:

*"You know, despite our experience, our education, and what our parents taught us, look at us, eating breakfast on the sidewalk, and spreading our luggage in the street."*

*"Exactly! You're so right!"* I reply smiling with some arugula between my teeth. It hasn't crossed our minds that we too must have given them the same vibe with our unusual breakfast setting.

The funny man then explains how they left the campground in a hurry this morning and did not want to make much noise and disturb the neighbors with the tent dismantlement and the packing. They just took everything and piled it all up into the car. So, now they take everything out, fold, pack and arrange accordingly back into the car. It's very nice of them to justify their morning activity, although we find nothing wrong with it. We rather appreciate the interaction. When we leave the parking lot, they are still going at it, but we have the pleasure of meeting them again later in the day.

Groups, families, and couples have already crowded the trail. Each of them has their rhythm, their colorful sportswear and healthy attitude. I have never seen so many older people dressed in sports apparel until this summer. Back home in Romania, old people don't hike, and their wardrobes are mostly from the last decade. A few lucky ones travel with their kids while babysitting the grandchildren. Otherwise, I don't have one memory of a family of three generations having a common activity during a vacation apart from enjoying a meal.

However, here, you can find this family portrait all over, and it is a given. The group moves at the pace of the slower ones - grandkids, grandparents, or mothers carrying infants. They usually choose short and easy trails for most of the members' enjoyment. This way they share a common memory and all have a story to tell. I appreciate a culture where old age is not kicked out the door but rather included in an active way of life.

We pass all the many families that will most likely stop at Landscape Arch (the third one on the trail and the most famous of all) and walk at a steady pace along with other couples and young gangs. It is still early morning, and the trail is ten miles long with quite an elevation to it. The sun is already burning as if its life depends on it. I skipped my usual hiking tank top today, opting for one of M.'s white t-shirts. In the hopes that white reflects the heat.

For a couple of hours, we encounter the most incredible stone structures sculpted by the same duo - weather and time—shaping them into perfect arches. They are among the things that are so hard for me to understand just like all the hoodoos, mesas, and buttes I've met along the North American desert. This place teaches me a lesson on the infinite strength of nature and its limitless creativity. Being in this corner of the world, where there is nothing to say, just see and listen, I admit that everything around me exceeds all human comprehension. This is now my new heritage, my most prized possession.

The trail follows a sand path that squeezes through and under impossible to reproduce boulders, and every mile or so it stops and gives way to another perforated cliff for us to gaze at in disbelief.

We pass by the Tunnel Arch and then the Pine Tree Arch. When we reach the Landscape Arch, we take a break for water and onomatopoeias, as this is the widest arch in the world. The latest measurements say it has a span of 290 feet, a height of 77 feet, a width of 18 feet, a thickness of six feet, and an opening of 295 feet. These are all highly impressive numbers!

Eavesdropping on a guide who passionately talks to a group of tourists about some unfortunate events that happened here, we find out that for quite some time nobody has been allowed under the arch. The last time people were under it, they heard an unusually loud thundering sound. They ran to take shelter close to the cliff while a compact piece of stone detached from the arch, crashed to the ground, and then rolled down the valley. They survived but were still afraid it will break in half by the looks of it. However, it did not break. Not then, and it has not broken during the last two decades. After that incident, the rangers diverted the trail and restricted access to the area underneath the arch.

The span of Landscape Arch is not the only reason for its fame but also its fragility and thinness. Geologists say either it is close to its end, or because of the lost weight, it still has hundreds of years to go. Regardless of the outcome, to be here now, able to admire it, is a privilege for me. Thank you, M., for bringing me to this exquisite park!

We then visit Double O Arch, Wall Arch, Navajo Arch, Partition Arch, and (right at the end of the route) a narrow, high, and dark rock formation called Dark Angel—speaking of bleak names in the western national parks. The rock is over 150 feet high and attracts professional climbers who consider it a challenge. It also attracts archaeologists because of the petroglyphs present on its walls. As in Capitol Reef, rangers don't promote this last aspect of the rock for the same good reasons. The information is out there due to social media, but only those who look carefully around the rock can find the engraved drawings. Near them is a sign that reads, "You've found something unique. Please preserve it." Quite impressive.

On the way back, we pass the same arcades. We intersect with groups that have just hiked up and see them for the first time, and we understand their reactions perfectly. The descent is easier only in theory. I already know it. That is why the four and a half miles back seem to be more difficult, longer, and hotter.

Right next to the Landscape Arch, we meet the couple from

the parking lot. We stayed for a quick chat and congratulated them on re-packing their luggage.

*"Good to see you again! So, where are you from?"*

*"Good to see you too! We're from Eastern Europe, Romania."*

*"Well, you're far away from home, aren't you? We're from Sacramento, California. We moved there to be close to the mountains and ski during the winter."*

*"That's really nice, being so close to the slopes."*

*"Well, you see, that's the thing about people... they are always changing their minds, and they are so hard to please. One day you buy a house just because from the backyard, you can see the mountains, but two years later, you realize you don't even notice them anymore. We did pretty much the same. Doesn't that make you wonder?"*

*"You're right, people are ungrateful like that, but it's a good thing they realize it."*

The discussion continues for a while on philosophical topics about human nature we had started in the parking lot. Then, we talk about the fact that we will soon arrive in California and climb Mount White, which deeply impresses the two. We say goodbye with handshakes and encouragement for a successful climb.

The Park is huge. Apart from the arches we've already seen, some are just as emblematic but in a different direction. We hop in the car and head to the first three arcades, North Window Arch, South Window Arch, and Turret Arch, which are about half a mile from the parking lot and close to one another. By the time I make it there, I am already barefoot. I change my T-shirt, and I am slowly coming back to life in the coolness of the air conditioning.

I am not even aware of how tired and exhausted I feel. When M. parks the car and tells me that we can now visit the other arches, something pops inside me, and I start crying uncontrollably. My new state of mind completely puzzles me. On one hand, I want to go see all the arches, because I am here and who knows if I will ever come back, and it is so beautiful. However, on the other hand, I refuse to leave the car when I remember the unimaginable heat outside. A mile would be easy-peasy under normal circumstances (even after the four miles I've already hiked today), but now I no longer feel capable.

The spectacle puzzles M., and he doesn't know how to handle what is happening. He doesn't understand whether I want to go another mile to the arches, or whether he should stay with me, or if he should go see them alone, or if I may calm down, we can see them together. I feel extremely silly in my childish tantrum, but I cannot control myself. Maybe the fatigue I have been accumulating over the past three weeks has caught up with me, because everything I did was difficult and extremely demanding.

Yes, I overcame obstacles and even overcame myself physically and mentally, which I am proud of, especially because at the end of each trail fantastic places were waiting for me. I am so happy to have seen them. But now, here, I have reached the end of my rope. I can't stop crying. I can't even get out of the car. M. reassures me and tells me it's okay, that he understands me. He has decided he will go by himself to see the arches and will bring me photos so I can see them too. I sit alone in the car, as my tears run out because of dehydration. I realize how absurd the situation is, especially for me. M. returns in less than fifteen minutes with incredible pictures and is curious to find out if I have regained my composure.

*"I'm better. I've calmed down. I'm just very, very tired. But I do want to go to the next arch together. I don't want to have any regrets, and I don't want to remember how I sat in the car and missed any of these beauties!"* I say, feeling idiotic about all of this.

We went together to visit the Double Arch, the highest in the park - practically a piece of a mountain 115 feet high and 145 feet wide, of which only two suspended stone strips remained. I am so happy I pushed myself out of the car.

*"Look! Another mile has not killed me, I am fine."* I say to myself.

Now, we have only the Delicate Arch left to visit, the emblem of the park, and the symbol of Utah. All the cars in this state wear its image on their license plates.

I am excited and ready for a new three-mile round-trip trail, but about halfway up the hill my body doesn't help me anymore. I almost fell. So, I retire from the race, this time without drama. Honestly, I want to, I tried, but I can't. I find a boulder in the shade and tell M. that he will find me here on his way back.

After less than ten minutes, a kid, maybe eight years old, comes and sits next to me on another boulder. He breathes hard and noisily as if he wants to attract my attention.

*"Hey, are you OK?"* I ask, starting the conversation.

*"Well, I guess. I'm fine, but it's so hot, and I'm bored."*

*"Yes, it's crazy-hot, I agree. That's why I took a break here in the shade."*

*"Me too. My parents are up there by that arch, but I told them I'm bored and that I'm going down. They should find me on their way back."*

*"So, how was the Delicate Arch?"*

*"You know, just like the rest of them. Fine, I guess, I don't know. Anyway, I don't understand it. Why do grownups have to do these things like walking around in the sand in the middle of the day when it's so hot? I just don't understand why they have to take me with them... I would have been better off waiting by myself in the car. Where it is cold. But no, I have to go with them to be bored all day..."*

I don't have time to reply to his rant, because his parents pass by us. I just say *"Goodbye. Nice to meet you!"* I shout, but he doesn't answer. He doesn't care about the arches or me; he just wants to get in the car and leave the heat behind. Honestly, so do I. Until M. returns, I have time to think about everything that today brought me, and I am reconciled with my decisions and with what I have already seen. More than satisfied. More than exhausted.

Leaving all the arches in the company of the other thousands of tourists, we then head to the exit of the park on the same road we came in at dusk. We pass the Balanced Rock, a stone structure that fully deserves its name, although nobody knows for how long. We realize it is one of the rocks from our sunrise photos from a few hours ago. We can't be wrong. We can't confuse such an outline. Almost 130 feet high, it looks like the Super Bowl trophy or like a football is standing upright on top of a milk bottle. That is just from the angle we see it now. The farther we go, the more it resembles E.T. with its disproportionate head, and then an Episcopal miter. In the pictures taken in the morning, it looks like an Arab seen from a profile, with his head wrapped in a turban. No matter how we look at it, it is a mystery how it keeps its balance with the considerable weight of the upper part.

There are four such rocks in the United States, all with the same name. Colorado, Idaho, Texas, and Wisconsin, each have one, each looking as if they are about to collapse and become just a pile of rocks. However, it can take a year or a hundred years for such an event to occur. Meanwhile, we win the lottery with the Balanced Rock in Arches.

The last few miles towards the exit are sprinkled with all sorts of hoodoos with human or architectural appearances. Some of which remain in my mind. In my camera, I've captured the Three Gossips and the Courthouse Towers.

We could stay here all week and maybe only then would we be able to see all that this park offers. Our journey now takes us far west, to Beaver, Utah, where we arrive at mile 5,895. Three and a half hours later. We stay in room 144 at the Quality Inn, where the bed is as comfortable as in all the hotels we have stayed so far and where sleep is better than at home.

I am so tired as if I plowed an entire field today. It is a new kind of burnout for me, which I love to feel in the bones and muscles of this body that carries me across America without giving up. If it were not in close relation to the head, the body would be capable of fantastic achievements. Today's events argue the sovereignty of the head over the body, forcing it to stop. I usually experience the opposite, when the mind convinces the body that it is capable, and it invariably is.

# CHAPTER VI - *NEVADA, THE SILVER STATE*

# 21 - *VALLEY OF FIRE STATE PARK, LAS VEGAS, NV*

T he same sun is in the sky today, although wrapped up in thick clouds of cotton candy. We head southwest for four hours, and it does not reveal any rays. Just as we enter Nevada, two rainbow pillars, among which the rain drags its torrent, frame the horizon. I feel, and I may be right, that we have caught up with the rain from Escalante. I imagine the rain is in love with traveling like we are, pouring its grace up and down across the desert. It seems unlikely that there would be more than one like it out there. We can't catch up with it until we enter the Valley of Fire State Park, but we find evidence of its passing along the way.

Nevada's oldest park is famous for its seventy square miles of red Aztec sandstone (Navajo sandstone's sister) mixed with gray and brown limestone. Truthfully, the first impression I have entering the park, and looking out of the car window at the mountains divided in two by the road, is that we are passing through hot coals. The landscape changes, taking us through a wide palette of pastels, stained in places with dark tones of gray and brick red.

Again, we choose a loop trail, to see as many of the park's attractions as possible, but we are quite skeptical about the weather. It is still overcast; the wind is hot and we seem to have the entire park to ourselves. We keep thinking about what to do, because the rain in these areas is dangerous. We don't want to get caught in a storm out on the trail. However, when we get to the parking lot and find a few more cars over there, we decide to stay and take the hike after all. We feel safer if there are other people around.

If we are lucky, the weather will not drive us away. We plan to do a loop trail that will take us past the White Dome, through the Pink Canyon, over the Fire Wave, and then finally back to the White Dome. It's three miles of walking in high atmospheric pressure and a heat emanated as if by a smoldering fire maintained under the earth's crust. It makes sense why they call it the Valley of Fire.

We are at peace with our decision. The landscape is fantastic and extremely familiar. As we have already seen so many expressions of the desert in the previous parks, we discover that many of them gather here as well. We pass by arcades, cross through canyons, climb hills of badlands of alien colors and textures. In the park's brochure, we read about the petroglyphs, ruins, and petrified trees discovered here, which complete the list of curiosities produced by the western North American desert, maybe except for hoodoos.

The Pink Canyon has a sandy path flooded in places with yesterday's rain, and there are parts we have to cross climbing its walls. I feel as if we are going through a raspberry cream puff pastry cake, powdered with instant coffee on top. We walk on sand, gravel, scree, and cliffs not yet perforated by torrents; through a canyon with walls that go up and down as we cross it, sheltering us with its height or exposing its folds of weathered rocks. The inside vegetation is impressive with delicate, tiny leaves, which I have to photograph up close to distinguish them individually.

We have a feeling of déjà vu arriving at Fire Wave. The red and white stone waves remind us of White Pocket. It is unbelievable how in the middle of this versatile park we meet such a replica. In an area of several thousand square feet of stone, surrounded by sand, cacti, dwarf shrubs, and endless mountains of embers, Fire Wave is the crown with which nature perfected the already convincing beauty of these places.

We are lucky to arrive dry back at the car, and as we head to the Valley of Fire Beehives (an incredible cliff resembling beehives) and Arch Rock, fresh sunlight floods us. The last pictures we take here are the most impressive, because the light brightens the colors in the chromatic mixture of the park, as salt brings out the flavors in food. Driving out of the park, we simply must stop a few times in the middle of the road and capture the meandering image it creates through the vastness of limestone and sandstone as if torn from a photography magazine.

The sun completely eludes the clouds until we reach Las Vegas at mile 6,170. It closely watches our every move up and down the Strip crowded with casinos, hotels, restaurants, malls, tattoo parlors, arenas, fountains, and lush gardens. We go in and out of air-conditioned casinos, where the air emanates cigarette smoke and room freshener, but it is much more breathable than the desert heat emanated from the hot asphalt.

I honestly like Las Vegas. One would describe it as a visual and auditory extravagance, a multicultural mixture seasoned with strong freedom of expression, a curiosity halt for anyone from anywhere, sitting in the middle of the desert and lit by a river of electricity. Bill Bryson captures its essence more artistically when he writes, *"I have never seen such a sight. It is an ocular orgasm, a three-dimensional hallucination, an electrician's wet dream"*[13].

We spent the night in Las Vegas and the next morning too. Then, we head northwest to Beatty, Nevada.

# 22 - *LAS VEGAS, BEATTY, NV*

We enjoy another overly serene morning on the streets of the fabulous Las Vegas, then a dark afternoon with clouds emanating gray heat. We stay cool in the car that takes us on deserted roads, bordered by spiky cacti of all heights and shapes, and billboards that compete in ingenuity and size.

I have noticed that, as we are nearing a city, the billboards are more frequent on the side of the road, and as we move away from Las Vegas, there are fewer and fewer. I remember the ones in Florida, where most of them advertise law firms, nursing homes, and physiotherapy clinics. In the desert, most of them show ads for fireworks, but the most impressive ones are 3D, with a cowboy hat, roller coaster rail, beach umbrella, or French fries coming out of the frame.

After a few tens of miles, we notice a storm breaking the sky in the direction we're going. Although rains are rare and eagerly awaited in the desert, they are not friendly at all when they come. We are fascinated by the image of the sky pouring into the horizon through a compact water curtain, and we arrive in Beatty right in the middle of the storm.

At mile 6,341, we check into Motel 6. We carry our luggage running through the puddles and into room 101, our home for the next two nights. After watching the water overflow on the other side of the window, I grab my book and read the last pages of *Wild* with justified satisfaction. Then, M. and I watch the movie *Wild* produced and played by Reese Witherspoon, who cannot live up to the novel written by Cheryl Strayed. In my opinion.

# 23 - *DEATH VALLEY NATIONAL PARK, NV*

W e find no trace of water in the morning when we go out in the parking lot, as if the earth had absorbed it to the last drop, quenching an unimaginable thirst. The sky is open, and in the air, there is still that moisture foreign to these places. It takes us half an hour to arrive in California at Death Valley National Park on the land of the Timbisha Shoshone tribe.

Car parts and ripped tires are scattered here and there on the side of the road. It seems that losing bits of their vehicle didn't attract the attention of focused or maybe tired drivers nor did it impede their locomotion. We're thinking that the heat exuded by the asphalt might have detached some secondary parts from the whole. All of this is crossing our minds because we're heading to the hottest place on the planet. Soon enough it will all make sense to us.

Entering the park, we noticed some cars painted in a black and white cameo pattern we had previously seen in the parking lot of the Motel 6 in Beatty. On our second morning there, we found out from the drivers who were having a smoke in front of the motel that the cars are the new Hyundai 2019 models. They had brought them to Death Valley to test in the heat. Certainly one of the tests is checking to see if there are parts in danger of falling off as it happened to the previously mentioned cars. I don't know what the outcome was, but I can tell you that our Subaru remained intact until delivering it back in Illinois. No ad intended.

We are in California, The Sunshine State, in the northern Mojave Desert, in the largest national park in the continental United States. It is the place that wins outright the scariest names competition, starting with the very name of the park: Death Valley; and then with some outstanding landmarks of the area such as Badlands, Badwater, Devil's Golf Course, Funeral

Mountains, and Furnace Creek. In total opposition, of name and appearance, you can visit places like Artist drive, Rainbow, Mosaic, and Golden Canyons, and each one is faithful to the name it bears for aesthetic, chromatic, or historical reasons.

Besides being the largest, it is also the hottest and driest national park in the United States. A land of contrasts in which mountains with snowy ridges border a completely arid scenery during drought with multicolored flora after the rare storms. A depression found at 282.2 feet below sea level recorded the highest temperatures on earth, 134°F in 1913, and the longest period in which the temperature did not fall below 129° F.

Apart from these impressive climatic details and a unique landscape, the park has a rich history with tentacles that stretch in the sphere of culture, civilization, and the paranormal. One more thing: Death Valley was the setting for over twenty-five movies, including Star Wars (filmed in 1977) and a few movies starring Gregory Peck and Marlon Brando.

There is often talk of *"death by GPS"* in this area, when Google Maps or GPS devices guide visitors to dangerous or non-existent routes. Due to low signal or location errors, many tourists find themselves in the middle of the desert with an empty gas tank in heat of over 115 °F; with no idea where they can find help in this 5,270 square mile park, in which only small areas are arranged for the public. Because M. knows that he can't rely on GPS in these vast uninhabited territories, every night he downloads the maps from Google Maps in advance for our next destination.

You have to be reckless to rush onto unmarked roads in a place that is rightly called Death Valley. Upon entering the park, information panels warn tourists of many dangers and advise them to have enough gas to return, enough water to hydrate, and not to be more than a few hundred yards away from the car at all times. The same tips await all travelers at each panoramic point.

For obvious reasons, we don't intend to walk too much on foot, especially since it is 115 °F, which is difficult to bear for over twenty minutes. We visit the Badwater Basin, where we are below sea level, (the second-lowest point in the western hemisphere after the Laguna Del Carbón in Argentina), and part of the Salt Flats, the park's saline area. But, we do stop at a few vistas where, in ideal climatic conditions, you could admire the mountains, hills, valleys, canyons, and dunes of salt and sand. Unfortunately, we can hardly distinguish them right now through the milky atmosphere still humid from last night's storm.

An interesting stop is the Furnace Creek Inn, which stands out from all the surroundings. It is a historic hotel embraced by an oasis of palm trees and flowers, at the foot of Funeral Mountains, overlooking the salt flats and the Panamint Mountain Range. Its inauguration, in 1927, marked the transformation of Death Valley from a wilderness into a national park.

We drive tens of miles inside the park while researching the unusual events and phenomena that have taken place here. Most revolve around survival, death, and sliding stones. The long list of people who made Death Valley an exotic tomb began before our era, when ancient tribes lived here. The few facts that are known about them speak of a population of giants.

Several archaeologists and explorers have said, over the past few centuries, that they discovered a system of caves and catacombs under Death Valley and remnants of an ancient civilization, but none of them has been able to find them on a later date. Most of them ended up dead on the park's tangled paths, and their bodies were never found. The Timbisha Shoshone tribe inhabited these lands for 1,000 years, and they left behind legends of these places being covered in an oasis of greenery and life. Then, begins the history of the white man.

In 1849, during the gold rush, some groups of searchers wanted to take a shortcut to the mines of California Mountains instead of the most travelled route. What they didn't know was that they were trading a shorter distance for an unmarked and untamed area. It's hard to believe that you can overcome such an eccentric climate and a misleading terrain with an ox-drawn cart. Only they didn't know what they were getting into. The examples are many and tragic. These events mark the moment when the area earned its well-deserved name. Those who survived remained here to exploit the gold, silver, and borax mines they found. By 1911, about 20,000 people were living in the area in actual cities with churches, saloons, shops, hotels, medical offices, and theaters. All that remained from these cities are a few ruins, abandoned mines, and the theater turned into a hotel that is said to be haunted. It's amazing how much tumult and how much history a place with no hint of domestic appearance can have.

We stopped for lunch at the Badwater Saloon in Stovepipe Wells Village. From the entire menu, I choose tortilla soup and *fondito*, which are surprisingly the same thing. Both are a kind of cheese sauce paired with tortilla chips. I dared to ask the server when I would get my soup, but apparently, I had already eaten it! Good thing I asked. Otherwise, I would have left with the impression that they accidentally brought me two portions of the same dish.

On the way to the motel, we stop to buy some Snapple, Sheryl Strayed's favorite lemonade during her trip on the Pacific Crest Trail in 1993. Just before we park the car, we have to yield to a family of wild donkeys, a mother and a foal taking their time crossing the street. I start reading *Waking Up in a Tent*[14], and after a few pages, I fall asleep for the next thirteen hours.

# CHAPTER VII -
## *CALIFORNIA, THE SUNSHINE STATE*

# 24 - *ANCIENT BRISTLECONE PINE FOREST, MOUNT WHITE TRAILHEAD, CA*

W e wake up slightly stiff from a short-coma-kind of sleep after twenty-three full and intense days. We have breakfast across the street at Denny's, where I have potatoes, vegetables, and eggs covered in cheese, straight from a sizzling pan. M. is a professional at choosing from menus with over twenty dishes and he invariably chooses sandwiches with a low risk of dripping egg yolk on his shirt. I always take the risk and rarely set off with an immaculate T-shirt. Especially if we have breakfast at a restaurant that serves me easy eggs.

After months of anticipation, it is finally the day before The Day we have been waiting for. Today, we stock up on sandwiches from the Subway across from Denny's before we head to White Mountain, California. On the front door, there is a No shirt, No shoes, No service sign. This makes me think that barefoot and bare-chested individuals must come here often for sandwiches. Fascinating places!

We soon follow in the footsteps of Sheryl Strayed through a few towns she had passed around the Sierra Nevada Mountains and their snowy paths in the middle of summer. Entering Lone Pine at 6,645 miles, we discover a small and chic mountain resort people refer to as The Gateway to the High Sierras. It is the portal to Mount Whitney (14,505 feet altitude - the highest point in the United States except for Alaska) and Mount Williamson (14,380 feet), the highest mountains in California. Soon after, we passed through Independence and Big Pine. These two cities run parallel to the PCT[15] with the Sierra Nevada to the west and the Inyo National Forest to the east.

In Big Pine, we leave the main road and turn right toward Ancient Bristlecone Pine Forest, the oldest forest on the planet. California has the forests with the oldest, tallest, and largest trees in the world. We have the honor to see all of them in the coming days, starting with the oldest forest inhabited by pine trees over

5,000 years old.

The Visitor Center is at an altitude of 10,500 feet, where we reach on an asphalt road. The forest stretches up to 11,150 feet, an impressive altitude for the survival of any form of vegetation. Except for the Bristlecone pines.

At the Visitor Center, we ask the ranger for information about accessing Mount White, and he only gives us good news. The road, although unpaved, is accessible by car up to 12,140 feet of altitude where the trailhead is located. The mountain is almost entirely snow-free, the ranger assured us. This is what we hoped for since M. relied on it being like this when designing the entire trip.

We begin the ascent to the most exciting adventure of my life, but I am not yet aware of that. As usual, I still don't know what I am getting into, but I rely on M. He knows better.

We drive up hundreds of feet in elevation on a dirt and gravel road with the bristle-cone-pine-forest spread over all the surrounding peaks. Before entering Route 168 to White Mountain Road, we take a quick detour to Bristlecone Pine Forest Scenic Byway and reach Patriarch Grove. The parking lot is full. Everywhere we look individuals with tripods and bulky cameras come from or head to the Cottonwood Loop Trail, a half-mile trail among the most contorted conifers I've ever seen.

It is remarkable how this forest can survive such high altitude and harsh climate, but what is even more unusual is the sandy soil in which it has been deepening its roots for the last 5,000 years. Because of the strong mountain winds and the birds hovering over the fir trees, the seeds have minimal chances to sprout and grow into a fine new tree. The forest is not dense, and the old patriarchs seem to be the same age.

In many of their trunks, two different trees seem to coexist, one dead and one alive. The general appearance of the tree itself is that of a bundle of tightly woven fibrous branches, some of which are full of green buds and cones, and others are completely dry or even charred.

At this height, the storm is one of the fashion designers with the strongest impact on nature. They leave the impression that in their anatomy you can distinguish lightning and thunder as eccentric accessories. The smell emanating from these ancient beings is something I will not soon forget. It is impossible. Millions of fragrant cones fill up the powerful mountain air with a strong fir scent. I'd like to bottle the scent in a receptacle, or rather absorb it into my skin and let it emanate among people.

We climb for more than an hour and a half until we reach the trailhead at 12,140 feet of altitude. The road stops in the middle of a wide plateau where there are only a few other cars parked, a tent, and a public toilet. We choose a place for our tent and start setting it up so that we'll have a roof over our heads before nightfall. Especially since the sky is suspiciously dark and the temperature is close to 50 °F. The lowest so far.

We put on an extra layer of clothes, and then sit on a log in front of the tent to have dinner, watching the hustle and bustle in the parking lot. A few young people, who came here to paraglide, have a flat tire and no spare. They talk about what to do and how to approach the descent to Bishop, where they are from. M. joins in the conversation and tries to help them with advice since we have nothing else to offer. Other people, who come down from Mount White at this hour, notice the group in need, and offer help.

It impresses me how kind people are to each other up here. I love them for their friendliness and for the positive attitude they have dealing with this situation. After extensive debates, a woman who has an extra seat in her car takes two of the young people to drive them down the mountain. This way the car with the flat tire will be lighter going downhill. The other two, who are stuck with the limp car, will have to drive slowly and keep inflating the bad tire as often as necessary until they make it home. I have to mention that their tone is calm and understanding. No one gets angry. No one blames anyone. There's no whining or moaning.

There are two other tents in the clearing, besides ours, and one of them has a portable shower cabin. At one point, two more cars appear, out of which four people emerge and immediately start setting up two tents. The four of them talk to the shower cabin man, and from their loud conversations, we find out that he had just climbed Mount White as practice for the ascent of Mount Whitney.

It is getting dark and the few random raindrops here and there are easy to ignore. Marmots and chipmunks search for food or burrows on the meadow where we set up the tent. It is quite cold and dark, so I retreat to the tent and sleeping bag to read a few more pages by flashlight. Lying down, relaxed, I notice that breathing is not as voluntary as I have always known it. Theoretically, I may not cope with the altitude tomorrow, but if I survived this long at this altitude, I should be fine. Overnight acclimatization will do me good.

M. stays outside for a while. The clouds have dissipated, and he can finally see the open sky. Just as he remembers, the stars have the same unmistakable geometry. He calls for me and I join him. We stargaze together for a while marveling at how close the stars are to the ground. If we were any taller, we could touch them with the tip of our nose.

# 25 - *MOUNT WHITE SUMMIT, BIG PINE, CA*

R ight at the conception of this trip M. informed me that at some point we would climb a tall mountain. This is why I trained for eight months as a wannabe Ironman Triathlon medalist. First, I had to recuperate from a torn meniscus and ACL surgery that I'd had last year on my right knee. Then, I had to recover and get in shape for everything that has been waiting for me so far and especially for today. I have been working out more this past year than in the last ten combined. Whoever said that muscles have memory was right, because my almost forty-year-old muscles remembered the twenty-year-old ones and made an average I can rely on.

Initially, we were supposed to climb Mount Whitney. Fortunately, we didn't win the lottery. Yes, I mean I was lucky not to challenge myself on the tallest mountain in the contiguous United States. But this didn't mess with M.'s plans one bit. Five minutes later, after the polite refusal from the lotteries of the American mountains, M. found another big, high, famous mountain to climb. If Whitney is 14,505 feet high, the lucky replacement, Mount White, is 14,252 feet, just 250 feet less.

Anyway, I didn't mind the changes. M. kept telling me that Mount White is so boring, so easy to climb, just a wide road accessible by bikes. It became clear for me that I would climb it, boring and simple as it is. Therefore, it made no sense for me to check the difficulty or duration of the trail, because if it was indeed so boring, easy, and simple, there was no need.

As you know, I haven't been interested in any other trail details from the long list of destinations in M.'s meticulously planned spreadsheet. I counted on my relatively youthful body and M.'s confidence that I am capable of it all. Under these circumstances and in this rhythm, we had hiked almost a hundred miles so far.

Even so, the trial hike we did yesterday evening didn't worry me, not even for a second, although I couldn't breathe easily on a mild ascent trail. I was aware we had reached 12,150 feet of altitude and that breathing was a problem. Still, I fell asleep thinking that today I will climb to the top of the most boring mountain, the third highest in California. Strangely, not even this ranking raised questions in my mind. However, I am a person of astonishing naivety, a fact repeatedly confirmed on this trip.

The alarm goes off at four in the morning. We wake up without a fuss, like two soldiers accustomed to the early hours of army life, the way we have been doing for the last twenty-five mornings. We put on warm clothes because it is under 40 °F. We take down the tent and pack the sleeping bags while chipmunks go around us, curious and nosy. Then, we have breakfast on top of the cooler by the light of the tent lamp.

We pack four liters of water each, beef jerky, apples, and hazelnuts. We lock the car hoping that the marmots won't eat the coolant lines, as we overheard some campground neighbors say that they do, lured by the smell and taste of coolant.

At 5:08 am, we are on our way. The sun is getting ready to come out from behind another mountain, tinted with purple, orange, and intense yellow. We leave silence behind us, over the three tents and the shower cabin. No sign of movement, not even a snore.

After this administrative preamble, my story begins, simple and boring, but not as I have imagined it until now. I am full of enthusiasm, ready to enjoy the scenery, to chirp when the sun casts its first multicolored rays over the wide and easy path that can be climbed even by bicyclists, to take photos of its astral glory, then to hike quietly and safely toward the top of the third highest California mountain peak. All this euphoria lasts for less than 300 feet, after which I realize that the difficulty of breathing I felt last night now amplifies with each step. To move forward, I have to breathe twice as deeply as I normally do. After literally counting a hundred steps, I have to take a break, lean forward with my hands on my knees, take another deep breath

173

until I calm down, and then do it all over again. I experiment on my own body how the lack of oxygen can turn it into a useless piece of meat.

I am determined to reach the top but I will need a strategy to succeed. I apply the Zion pattern and design a plan of a hundred steps + break. Then later fifty steps + break + sitting on a boulder. Finally, towards the end, twenty steps + break + throwing myself on whatever is closest.

I constantly try to breathe as deeply as I can, but I still feel dizzy at times. I say nothing because it is extremely difficult for me to recover the wasted air. Therefore, I don't even complain. I moan; I go bananas, and refrain from explaining to M. in colorful details how hard and nearly impossible it is for me to do this extreme sport. So, I climb 100-50-20 steps at a time, up to 14,250 feet.

In all this monotonous strategy, I find the element of simplicity and boredom of the trail after all. Despite everything, I am firmly convinced that I will reach the summit even at this pace. No matter how long it takes.

Just as I begin to comfort myself and become my own cheerleader for the many hours ahead, a red-haired man, dressed in shorts and a T-shirt passes us by running and says, *"Hi, how are you? Isn't it a beautiful day?"* I answer nothing. I treasure the air that has been accumulating in my lungs with such effort, but M. agrees with him and wishes him a wonderful day.

No, this meeting doesn't discourage me at all. Why would you think that? It has the potential to humiliate me and my turtle-like locomotion compared to the aforementioned man who's sprinting like a prairie coyote. But it doesn't. Moreover, the man asks us if we want to take a selfie with him, and we can't refuse. He is far too happy, so we don't want to ruin that for him. We step closer together and smile as we see fit. The boys with wide smiles and their teeth in sight. Me with clenched lips for fear of losing even a drop of air from my lungs.

About two miles from the trailhead, we find a research center belonging to the University of California. We read more about it online the next day. It studies the impact of altitude on sheep pregnancies, besides meteorology and other less interesting topics. Certainly, our sprinting friend works there, considering we have not seen him back at the campground, and he doesn't have any mountain equipment. Not even a bottle of water. He seems excessively familiar with the trail.

While I gasp and crawl, M. always looks rested, always waiting for me. He walks, looks back, and sees me overturned on some rock, or leaning on my knees. Every time, without exception, he tells me, *"You are doing great. Come on. We're almost there!"* although there are still seven miles to go. Then five. Then three. When there is only one left, he yells happily, *"Come on. We're there!"* Although I've had to take breaks every ten steps during this last mile.

We make an excellent team, M. and I. ME, a mountain marmot with turtle-like pace, and HIM, a bighorn-mountain-sheep who could probably climb the trail twice while I would climb only once. I see him hopping and sprinting on the boring path, smelling red, yellow, and white flowers, politely greeting other fellow travelers, marmots, and chipmunks. He encourages me all the time and trusts me. He tells me how well I am doing, although I honestly think I am a pathetic sight. But, he is truly happy for me when he takes a picture of me on top of Mt. White, holding the altitude sign.

I sit up there, very high up, and it seems so natural for me to be there after nine miles of constant hiking and five hours of sweat, cold, snot, and some repressed tears. What is difficult for me might be a walk in the park for others (for example for M. and that red-haired man who was jogging up the mountain this morning). I have to tell you that as we were still going up, he was already descending. Shirtless. By the time we were coming down, he was climbing back up, but this time on his bike!

Nonetheless, I proudly announce that I have just climbed my own Everest!

To be honest, throughout the climb, I had several moments of total confusion. All sorts of questions and answers popped into my head.

*"Who made me do this?"*

*"Why am I doing this?"*

*"I will never do this again!"*

*"It's good I'm doing it now so I don't have to do it again!"*

*"But, why do I have to do it anyway?"*

It is as if I have a representative of both good and evil on each shoulder, who bring pros and cons to all these questions. After each round of answers, everything balances out. It all comes down to the fact that I drew myself into this situation and to the well-known truth that without effort you cannot accomplish anything. In this case, the equation is extremely simple: without effort, I cannot reach the top. I am aware of this truth; I own it, and in a rather masochistic way, it makes me happy.

I think of Paula, a friend who asked me a few weeks ago why I would do such a thing. I probably replied with some random words like beauty, picturesque, adrenaline, flora, fauna, memories, perseverance. However, in pursuing this ascent, I have the palpable feeling of being capable of much more than I think I am. I believe people are capable beings in general but sometimes only under circumstances that require patience, endurance, perseverance, and complete self-denial.

This entire experience, including the nine miles back, seems unreal to me. As I was going downhill, I was remembering how the summit appeared to me, how far up, how untouchable and unreachable. How ultimately impossible for me to have been there, to have breathed those gray clouds that invaded the tip of the mountain, and to have written my name into the record book. This tremendous difference between reality and my level of accepting reality makes me believe that the human being is a wonder.

Equally fascinating to me is my attitude downhill when the hardest part was over. We cross paths with groups on their way up, and it takes me one look at them to know that they're in the same boat I was while climbing up. They are exhausted and some of them can barely breathe. Just like me. Then, I hear myself telling them cheerfully, *"There, there, you're doing well!"* As if I have already forgotten my struggle when I could not breathe and walk at the same time for over ten steps. Such arrogance! And, all this had happened barely an hour earlier.

We, humans, are very twisted! I was also thinking of M., who had categorically told me I could make this journey. His conviction had become my truth, which I could not contradict no matter how difficult it might have turned out to be for me. We truly are amazing beings!

I breathe easier on my descent, maybe because there is less physical effort, maybe because the happiness and pride of having climbed so high propel me, or maybe because now I can notice the landscape of this not-so-boring mountain. The summit with the University of California's cabin, the scattered patches of snow, and the register in which my name and M.'s appear next to July 15, 2018, are behind, getting farther and farther away. I finally jumped for joy. Metaphorically.

In all directions, marmots and chipmunks romp around and disappear underground as we get closer. I take a longer break halfway down the mountain. Overturned on a boulder, I breathe deeply as if a doctor is checking my lungs with a stethoscope. A marmot in its entire alpine splendor shows up a few feet from me. This sight makes me hold my breath, for fear I might scare it away. I try to catch M.'s eye, who is about 200 feet ahead and make him turn around without creating too much commotion. He joins me shortly after, and we enjoy the show together.

We stand still and watch the furry animal and I think it's doing the same thing. It keeps getting closer and closer until only two or three feet separate us. Unfortunately, a couple we met up on the peak passes by, and our friend disappears among the rocks while we greet each other. We later find out that they call it the yellow-bellied marmot. It will become a character we often remember and talk about.

White, red, yellow, and purple flowers gather in compact bouquets to border the trail. M. shows me in the distance two gray coyotes, probably out hunting marmots or cottontail rabbits. A little further down, a wild black horse with a star on its forehead prances around as if to lure us to do the same. I can only crawl with my boot laces unwound and my toes flattened from too much downhill. We pass the university buildings and notice, in a covered enclosure, a flock of sheep and dozens of marmots and chipmunks sneaking in and stealing their food. But, I can't give this too much thought or wonder why they chose sheep and not goats or pigs for the experiments, because every bone in my body wants to give in and drop me by the side of the road. I need extra strength to keep them all together. Nevertheless, when our green car appears in my field of vision, all of my fleeting sufferings lose intensity.

The serene sky entwines with strong shades of storm ready to thunder, and the air is so fresh you can almost bite it. We are so lucky the rain has bypassed us and that I have made it back in one piece. All the muscles and bones listed in the biology book hurt, but I forget the pain when I see myself in the car with this experience beautifully wrapped in an unreal memory.

As we take off our sweaty layers of waterproof clothing and peel off our boots and socks, which in the last ten hours have become one with the epidermis, an elderly woman approaches us with that American familiarity that I cannot get enough of. She asks us if we have just descended from the summit, if there is still snow, and if the trail is in good shape. She and her husband want to climb to the last patches of snow, where they should find a certain blue flower, which blooms only in summer after the snow melts. They are from Sacramento, and they come here every year hoping they will photograph this flower. Last year they came too late. Maybe they are lucky now. We wish them the best of luck, but M. advises them to climb tomorrow morning because now it is already late and the sky doesn't look promising. It's a known fact that in the mountains it rains almost every day in summer.

And he is right. On the way back to Big Pine, just as we pass the Visitor Center, it starts hailing, but this rain seems to pour only here on the mountain. Everything is dry and hot in the city.

We have dinner at Country Kitchen in Big Pine, after we take out almost all the contents of the car in the parking lot, looking for M's phone. Our effort to extract parts from the car is in vain, because the phone is exactly where it should be. However, being so tired or not paying much attention, we don't spot it from the beginning. We are tidier than the couple from Arches though and don't overflow onto the sidewalk.

Then, we hide full-bellied in lair number 11 in Bristlecone Motel, thinking of our new friend, the yellow-bellied marmot.

# 26 - *MONO LAKE, MAMMOTH LAKES, BISHOP, CA*

The morning is glorious here, at the foot of the over 13,000-foot-tall mountains, and the small tourist town enchants us once again as we cross it going to Country Kitchen for breakfast. The place is quiet for now, just like us. A few people sit in the next booth, and three old men at the bar. The diner resembles every other diner we have stopped by in the West so far. Paneled walls loaded with paintings or photos of animals or landscapes of the area, shelves with random vintage objects and framed cute quotes. Sugar, ketchup, mustard, hot sauce, salt, pepper and a variety of at least three kinds of jam, all cram in small bottles and packets in caddies on every table. Instead of chairs, there are padded booths for two or four people. The servers are invariably nice to us and familiar as if they have always known us.

The three old men at the bar seem to be the diner's regulars, because after they finish their breakfast and coffee, they stand and go to wash their cup at a sink behind the bar and then leave the restaurant cup in hand. I find this unusual habit extremely adorable, as I do the three friends, one white, one Latino, and one black.

M. eats his eggs Benedict, and I eat my veggie version of the same dish. We decided that before proceeding with today's plan we should drive up to the Sierra View Observation Site, a panoramic point from where you can see the Sierra Nevada Mountains lined up across the entire horizon. As yesterday was pouring rain when we were coming down to the city, we could not enjoy this astonishing view. Today, however, it is quite clear, and this observation site is the ideal place for contemplation and morning coffee consumption.

The day is waiting for us in spectacular aquatic places, which will hydrate our map and cool it down after all the desert scorching heat. We pass by Bishop and then by Lee Vining, the town where the characters from Waking Up in a Tent end their journey, long before the end of the PCT. The story is simple yet impressive: a couple in their sixties read *Wild* together and decide to walk as much of the PCT as they can, just like Cheryl Strayed.

Shortly before Lee Vining, we visited Mono Lake. I believe they should call it a roofless-cave-lake with its fantastic looking stalagmites shooting out of the water in all directions. I saw images of these stagnant waters perched at almost 6,500 feet of altitude on the internet but I couldn't wait to admire them in person, just to make sure they are real. And they are.

We approach the lake from several directions until we find one that will take us closer to the shore, to South Tufa Point. There are several vistas around the lake from where you can admire the mirror of the water pierced by what we soon discover to be hundreds of *tufas*. For me, it is not enough just to see it. I want to understand what I'm looking at. In the Visitor Center, we are acquainted with what a tufa is, as much as our abilities to digest geological explanations allow us. What remains with us, after an entire museum and many explanatory panels, is that they represent petrified springs.

We walk barefoot on the sandy shore, and from time to time, we wade into the water up to our ankles for a complete experience. We intersect with a herd of wild geese, a few seagulls, and dozens of other tourists.

Interestingly enough, the geological formations have not always been visible. It wasn't until around sixty years ago that they began rising to the surface. After the California Department of Water and Electricity diverted the lake's waters through an aqueduct 300 miles to the south the water level diminished. Once the tufas were in plain sight, explorers and environmentalists in the area realized the antiquity and richness of this lake and fought to save and protect it. Already halved in depth (160 feet) and surface (seventy square miles), they discovered some unusual facts. Apparently, the underground springs emit calcium carbonate into the lake water, which then forms the limestone turrets, some almost thirty feet high. This phenomenon happens only in nine other places in the world. The water gets twice as much saline as compared to the ocean. The high alkalinity of its waters makes it impossible for fish to survive in the lake, but it is beneficial to a unique shrimp species that yearly attracts many kinds of migratory birds.

Mono Lake is an ecosystem where millions of birds nest each year, a scientific center, and an unearthly view that attracts tourists from all over the world. We leave with our eyes full of blue sky, clouds of goose down reflected in transparent green waters, white sandcastles with steep turrets, and green-fleshy vegetation all around.

I don't know what else I could see today that would increase the feeling I already have of winning the lottery, but Mammoth Lakes brings its own beauty to the table and doubles my profit. This is a mountain resort in California, at 7,881 feet of altitude. I could stay here for a month in summer and one in winter. No doubt about it. Nature endowed it with ski slopes and cross-country skiing trails, lakes, waterfalls, and hot springs. Man's hand also contributed to this feast of natural riches, building hotels, restaurants, shops, chalets, cottages, cabins, and campgrounds for biannual vacations throughout the resort.

We choose trails that will take us in different directions to see as much as possible of the area. We visit Lake George, Lake Barrett, Lake Mary, and Twin Lakes with their overlaid waterfalls. From one lake to another, we pass by cabins you can rent together with a pontoon and a boat. There are huts with wide terraces where you can relax and melancholically watch the pine forest-framed lakes and mountain ridges; and campgrounds that have "No vacancies" signs at the entrance.

The cars coming in or out of the park have bicycles and kayaks strapped or mounted on them. From place to place, groups of anglers wait under the wide brims of their hats to catch something good to put on the grill tonight. To our surprise, we also see some chic fisherwomen who turn fishing into a fashionable activity.

Children lick ice creams, young people jog, discreet couples pedal boats, and tourists of all ages go up and down the trails between the lakes. They then have dinner outside the eatery. Groups of middle school girls sit in picnic areas and whisper about the cute boys in the camp. M. and I walk past them all, smiling widely.

What to do first: breathe in the fresh air; take pictures of the mountains, lakes, forests, and wild colorful flowers; sunbathe on the shore; wade in the water? We do them all. Leaving the resort, we pass under bridges and gondola lines, past the ski slopes, and then past the town of Mammoth Lakes, where over 8,000 lucky people live.

At mile 6,990, we reach Bishop and have the misfortune to eat the most awful dinner of this journey. After twenty minutes of elaborate study of the restaurant list in the area, Aaron Schat's Road House is the winner. We follow the advice of avid reviewers who had given the place gave ***** on TripAdvisor and order onion rings, garlic parmesan fries, and ribs. The ribs are cold and undercooked. Therefore, we indulge in onion rings and French fries dipped in blue cheese dressing, too happy to make any complaints after such an amazing day.

We spend the night in room 117 of the Travelodge, Bishop.

# 27 - *YOSEMITE NATIONAL PARK, FRESNO, CA*

W e are currently in California, the Golden State. The morning to which the alarm wakes us up is as bright as the waves of the Pacific Ocean at sunset. That is how I am imagining them now, as the ocean is getting closer but is not yet in sight.

In M.'s spreadsheet, today is Yosemite National Park Day and our expectations are at a respectable height. M. has not been here before either, so, visiting the park, which exhales the poetry of nature through its name and two impressive cliffs, El Capitan (the mecca of professional climbers) and Half Dome (the ultimate challenge for amateur climbers) will be a first for both of us.

We leave Bishop and head northwest with the Sierra Nevada mountains on the left and the Inyo National Forest surrounding us. In Lee Vining, we turn left and in a few tens of miles, we enter Tioga Pass, the highest pass in the US, on California Route 120. We are at 9,943 feet of altitude as indicated on the marking at the right side of the road, and we are bathing in a full alpine landscape.

As we approach Yosemite, we feel as if we are in a commercial advertising the park. We are the target audience as well as the actors of this ad. The car slides silently on the winding highway; the red and yellow flowers on the side of the road sway in the summer wind. The lake we pass picturesquely reflects the pine forest that outlines it, and invisible fish jump over the smooth surface of the water drawing intermittent circles that disappear in a blink of an eye. The lakeside campground is just waking up. Multicolored tents covered with dew, hammocks tightly joining sturdy pine trunks, people preparing breakfast as steam comes out from under the lid of a pot that balances on a camp stove create an idyllic portrait of the national park. All that is missing is the soundtrack. It first gently tickles our eardrums and as we drive deeper into the park it rises in decibels. Once we enter the Yosemite Valley, which welcomes us with intimidating ridges resembling an ancient cathedral pipe organ, the notes reach a musical climax.

Everything happens according to the script, except for the ending. The day is clear and golden, as I said earlier. However, inside the park, there seems to be a fog that visually blocks the upper half of the landscape. The most impressive part. We don't pay too much attention to it, and assume it will dissipate by noon. We locate ourselves on the map we received at the entrance and look for a parking lot. Just like Zion, travel within the park is done by shuttle, which takes four million tourists annually to over 200 trailheads. Yosemite is an expansive natural reservation, 1,169 square miles to be precise, and the third oldest national park in the United States. It became a natural reserve in 1890 and thirty-five years ago a UNESCO World Heritage Site.

The immensity of the park mesmerizes us, as well as the endless leisure possibilities from which we try to choose a few for our visit. At the same time, the indescribable crowd in the Visitor Center, the parking lots, shuttle stations, trailheads, and sidewalks discourages us. There are so many people per square foot that we imagine them hanging from the trees too. Not only are there many, but they come from every corner of the planet. Looking around it's like flipping through an atlas with images of all the peoples of the world. It's the first time on this trip that we gave a thumbs-down to a park because of congestion.

Patiently but with great difficulty, we find a spot for our car on a remote edge of one of the parking lots. Then we try to pick some trails from the park's abundant menu. There is plenty to choose from: lakes, waterfalls, rivers, Sequoia forests, historical sites, museums, climbing walls; swimming, paddling, fishing, observing wildlife, and bird watching. All trailheads are a few shuttle stops away, and the attractions spread between 2,000 and 13,000 feet of altitude, all packed with consistent percentages of annual visitors.

We choose four trails that end in three spectacular and popular waterfalls and one lake, probably because we can't grow tired of water after three weeks of blazing heat.

The first one is the highest waterfall in North America, Yosemite Falls. We can see as soon as we enter the path, hundreds of yards away. The view is magnificent and attracts us like a magnet despite the fog, along with hundreds of other tourists who admire it with the same astounded facial expressions. As we are getting closer, we realize that we have only seen the top of the waterfall. The forest at the foot of the granite wall blocks the bottom part. Arriving in front of it, onomatopoeias start jumping around on our tongues and we can no longer hear our thoughts, nor each other. Part of this happens because of the thundering noise produced by falling water from 2,425 feet up and the thousands of voices shrieking in all the languages of the world at the same time.

Wooden railings border the end of the trail creating a semicircle that faces the waterfall. Most tourists stop here to take pictures and rest. We want to see it more closely, in fact, as close as possible. So, we climb a few hundred yards of massive boulders until we reach the exact spot where the water flows into an emerald green natural pool. Looking around, we see dozens of other curious people climbing the rocks like spider-men. Some of them dive into the icy water.

We move along the Yosemite map and then climb to Vernal Falls. People of different colors, religions, cultures, and ages swarm up a wide steep trail for about three miles. Although the path ascends along a mountain wall, theoretically revealing more and more of the valley and the opposite wall, nothing is visible. All of it, the valley, the mountains, and the sky seem to hide behind a steamy window. When we reach the top of the waterfall, we notice how a matte red sun sits above the park without spreading light. It is not foggy. We later find out from the rangers that it is actually smoke. Several forested areas in the park are on fire, and the smoke is the one invading the valley and limiting visibility.

Despite all the inconveniences, we can see the waterfall well enough. We also feel it on our skin through the infinite cold drops that bounce from its slide. It echoes in our ears for another two hours after we descend, just like after a Metallica concert. In front of the waterfall, a voluminous and flat rock stands as a pedestal for several thousand pictures daily, including ours. A kind American hiker takes a few pictures of us. We do the same to other fellow travelers. We all take acrobatic poses on top of the rock, with the waterfall unraveling in the background. The imposing ridges of the surrounding mountains hardly show their faces through the smoke, but instead squirrels, deer, chipmunks, and bluebirds make up for it.

Next stop is Mirror Lake. The path that takes us there seems to be descending from a fairy tale, winding among long and freshly sharpened pencil-like pines, 2,000-year-old redwoods, fleshy ferns, and delicate colorful flowers. The lake awaits in a lively clearing where groups of visitors look thoroughly prepared for a day by the water. It is as if we have arrived at another resort, where the primary activity is chilling.

After about six miles of sustained hiking, we decide this is the perfect place for a long recess. We take off our boots and socks and take a few steps in until the water is just below the knees. We pass a few wild ducks with a bossy attitude. People, folding chairs, umbrellas, strollers, babies, kids, blankets, balls, coolers, badminton nets, and floats skirt the shore. There are crowded picnic areas, and smoke comes out of a few grills. The water becomes stingingly cold after about five minutes of dabbling, but the big rock in the middle of the lake invites everybody to do cannonballs. About ten brave and courageous ones wait in line, take turns to climb it, and jump boisterously into the lake.

Before leaving the park through the western exit, and then driving a hundred miles south, we stop to pay a visit to the Bridal Veil Falls. The waterfall's resemblance to a bride's veil is due to the wind that separates the flowing water from the mountain wall, making it flutter to the side as if gravity would not attract it to the valley. Here too, the path brings us to a fenced area with wooden railings from where you can admire the landscape together with dozens of other admirers of nature and weddings, but we want to go further into the landscape. We climb again a wide boulevard of boulders thrown by time under the folds of the waterfall. We lean right on the edge of the natural pool where M. spontaneously dives in. Numerous times.

*"The water is ok, come on in!"* says M., but I am quite taken with the free show that happens right before my eyes.

A Latino woman sits on a flat boulder and adopts various poses of a well-versed model while an Indian man takes pictures of her on request. She then checks out the photos, but her unhappiness with the outcome is palpable. Maybe the pose doesn't bring out her qualities, or maybe the Indian guy isn't familiar with a photo composition. Whatever it is, she stays there on the boulder. Waiting. After the author of the pictures puts on his shoes and leaves, she approaches another man, a little to the left. She probably has more confidence in his abilities, because he has a bulky professional camera hanging around his neck. He politely accepts the second-hand photographer job and begins the photo session with the woman now sitting on another boulder, in a mermaid-style position, with a wide smile and visible teeth. I try to convince M. to pose for me in a stork pose, but he prefers to plunge into the water, imitating a frog.

A hundred miles later, we turned up in Fresno, California. At mile 7,216, we park in front of the Best Western and carry our luggage up to room 273.

Sometimes, I have no choice but to reduce the story to numbers, because their values are increasing significantly. We are approaching 7,500 miles across the United States and 120 miles on foot throughout the national parks. We have been prancing around the map of the United States of America for almost a month, as two souls and travel experts joined by the beauty of nature. M. leads the way and I follow him with admiration and confidence. Maybe just by writing this book, I could prove my immense gratitude.

# 28 - *SEQUOIA & KINGS CANYON NATIONAL PARK, MORO ROCK, MONTEREY, CA*

T oday, the roads take us south, to Sequoia & Kings Canyon National Park, two parks in one enormous area of 722 square miles. We arrive in the Land of the Giants, which we visit with heads upside down and gaze lost in the sky. This is the birthplace of the famous sequoia trees, the most voluminous in the world. We felt the exotic taste of the forest as soon as we entered The Generals Highway, the road that leads to the park entrance, following State Route 198.

The Park is as old as Yosemite, protected by law since 1890. Before anyone discovered its value and fought to turn it into a nature reserve, it had been home to the Native American Mon-ackee tribe, who left behind traces in the form of petroglyphs found in several sites in the park. It also used to be a source of timber and building material for the first white people who came to the area. It is a classic story of shelter, and exploitation followed by preservation.

Shuttles are available here for tourists, but there are also enough parking places from where you can reach the important trails in the area. Strenuous parts of the famous Pacific Crest Trail and John Muir Trail cross the park at high altitude and dozens of other trails lead to waterfalls, lakes, rivers, and peaks in the Sierra Nevada Mountains. We limit ourselves to visiting the two leading generals today. General Sherman Tree and General Grant Tree.

Our quest starts with 1,700 years old General Grant, the second largest sequoia in the world. We find ourselves on the path behind a group of teens who are probably summer camping here. We heel them mainly because of the two teachers or guides dressed in *Role Model* T-shirts, who enlighten the bunch about Grant and the sequoia forest. We enthusiastically attend an interactive teaching session, in which the supervisors subtly allure the kids into a trivia game giving them the opportunity to learn something about the places visited during the vacation.

*"Look how huge it is! How many people do you think it takes to hold General Grant?"* asks one of the role models.

*"Five, ten, thirteen,"* the kids answer randomly.

*"Well, actually it takes twenty people with their arms wide open! Tell me this: why do you think they call it General Grant?"* the same adult goes on.

*"Because this is the name of the man who found it? Because it is so huge?"* some kid shouts.

*"Great answers! In fact, the eighteenth President of the United States proclaimed this tree as The Nation's Christmas Tree. Guess what his name was?"*

*"Graaaaant!"* Yell all the kids at once.

*"Yes! Ulysses S. Grant. At that time, they thought this was the largest tree in the forest but later discovered General Sherman,"* the teacher continues and then guides the group along the trail with us in tow.

We keep eavesdropping and find out that sequoias reproduce through seeds that can remain in cones for up to twenty years until something shakes them off. The factor that speeds up this process is fire. The heat forces the cones to open up and the seeds to fall to the ground. Thus, a new generation of sequoias will be born. The Park administration initially fought wildfires and tried to control them, but they discovered after decades of experiments that without fire the forest would not regenerate. After having this revelation, we notice that most of the sequoias look burned at the lower part of the trunk, and draw the conclusion that this happened intentionally. We see the same thing in the redwood forest a few days later.

General Grant owns 46,608 cubic feet and is 267 feet tall. General Sherman is even larger - 52,500 cubic feet and eight feet taller. It has been declared the largest tree in the world and the largest living thing/largest living entity/creature in the world.

We reach it after a walk on a paved path where parents push strollers and a few adults roll in wheelchairs. As in all parks here in the US, things are designed for the public to be accessible, to be pleasurable, and useful. The alleys take us to the foot of these gigantic trunks with their crowns lost somewhere in the stratosphere. Being in their presence, the predominant feeling I have is one of safety, and the instinct manifested by most visitors is to hug them. The place exudes health, strength, beauty, and eternal youth.

A wooden fence encloses General Sherman and the surrounding alleys, clearly to give the tree some space away from the curious and touchy crowds. In front of it, there is a queue of dozens of people waiting in line to take pictures with it. Even this seems common sense to me - to be given a chance to take pictures of the General, without risking being photo bombed in the process. To me, the respect for others is real here. In situations like this, I realize how much harmony it spreads, how peaceful living can be among people if given proper rules.

The light breaks through the tall canopy of foliage in fragmented sequences. The atmosphere is semi-obscure. From place to place, we see exhibits of sectioned sequoia trunks, roots and all, or even sections of it cut out in the shape of an arch that you can walk under without hunching. The dimensions are huge. Impressive.

In the park museum, The Giant Forest Museum, one can discover more about them: varieties, dispersion, heights, diameters, circumferences, leaves, cones, reproduction; the history of the people who lived here; who took advantage of the natural wealth and who protected the place. Apart from all that knowledge, I leave the museum with a pair of miniature sequoia stainless steel earrings.

Right across the road from the museum, a sequoia stricken by natural causes takes us by surprise and stops us in our tracks. The Tunnel Log got its title back in 1937. Because of its colossal length and weight, it is practically impossible to move. The rangers cut a piece of it as wide as the road and as tall as an off-road vehicle with a trunk box on top, still leaving a few feet of the log's thickness as a roof. We drive under it slowly and experience the spectacle of driving through a log turned into a tunnel.

In 1989, writer Bill Bryson travelled to this park specially to go through this particular tunnel tree, acting on a wish he'd had since childhood. His parents had received a postcard with the very image of this tree with a car passing through, and Bill reached adulthood with the desire to see it in person. During his journey through the American states, and writing about it in his book *The Lost Continent*, he drives hundreds of extra miles to make it here, but he does not find it and leaves disappointed. He later learns that such a tree would also be found in the redwood forests, hundreds of miles to the north. However, he can no longer make such a detour, and his childhood dream persists. If he'd had Google Maps at the time and access to social media, he would not have left without the experience of walking through a tree. There is indeed a redwood called Chandelier Tree, through which we will drive a few days later and which is not overturned, but very much alive and still standing.

We never leave a park without climbing something. That's a fact. For this occasion, we choose a dome-shaped granite rock that watches over the sequoia forest, over the valley that opens widely below, and over the Giants Highway, that winds its curves toward Three Rivers, California.

We climbed the 351 steps to the top of Moro Rock. Sadly, there is no unique view over The Great Western Divide to reward us as the brochure advertises. Instead, we find a polluted valley, and the information board at the end of the steep trail explains it. The pollution seems to come from Asia entering the continent through San Francisco Bay, and stopping at the foot of the 13,000-foot-high mountains. No matter how hard we squint at the scenery, we cannot increase the contrast of the image before us. What lays at the foot of this rock is a faded picture that makes us overly sad.

M. drives the car like paddling a boat over light waves, leaving behind the forests and the mountains and rolling over hills that seem to me either sunburned or covered in golden velvet. We pass Fresno and descend closer to the Pacific Ocean, among endless orchards. I'm thinking of the largest ocean on the planet I will soon encounter. M. knows it well and can't wait to address it in his special way.

*"How have you been my friend? I have missed you!"*

He's told me many times that the United States Pacific Coast is not how I imagine it. But, how could I imagine it really, other than endless beaches, sand, salt, sun, waves, and tanned blonde surfers? Once again, M. is right.

At mile 7,552, we record the first contact with its shores. The beautiful Monterey area should reveal the scenery of Big Little Lies, with coastline villas and lace waves edging the rocky rims. Instead, I see no shore, no rocks, no waves, and no ocean through the cotton wool fog that covers the whole of Monterey. No sign of Californian summer or golden state either. Sharp treetops difficult to identify pierce the fog, and if Google Maps didn't tell me where I am, I would think we are nowhere near an ocean. By the time we occupy room 107 at the Comfort Inn, I start feeling the salty ocean; actually, this is the only thing that convinces me of my whereabouts.

**29 -** *BIG SUR, HEARST SAN SIMEON STATE PARK, PIEDRAS BLANCAS ELEPHANT SEAL ROOKERY, THE HENRY MILLER MEMORIAL LBRARY, GARRAPATA STATE PARK, POINT PINOS LIGHTHOUSE, LAGUNA CREEK BEACH, SHARK'S FIN COVE, PIGEON POINT STATE HISTORIC PARK LIGHT STATION, HALF MOON BAY, CA*

T he next morning is a sibling of the previous evening. I don't know what to do with the enthusiasm that I have been progressively accumulating for the last thirty days. I've hoped to loudly express it at the sight of the ocean, like a pressure cooker suddenly uncovered, emanating steams of fervor. All I can do is mumble an expectation that will soon try my patience. I also have to mention that yesterday morning I imagined that today I would wear a sundress and a swimsuit underneath, to sunbathe and swim wherever we stop, but reality forces me to wear long pants, a jacket, and a tight scarf wrapped around my neck.

We drive a few tens of miles south to Big Sur and even further, with the full list of beaches and bays we want to see along the California Pacific Coast. But the highway is closed due to landslides. As the fog insistently surrounds us and accompanies us down the map, we give it a few hours to raise its imponderable steam at least a hundred feet above the water, and at least show us what lies beneath.

Indeed, apart from the bad luck, a serene day smiles down on us. From all the promised beauty from gulf to gulf, we only see a blonde curl or a turned eyelash. I say yes to whatever I'm given and put my imagination to work. We stop whenever the shoulder widens to the right into a vista point. We head to the steep edge, hoping that below it we will finally see waves, sand, and a distant horizon.

First, we see only the rocks that cut the bay, and the fog that covers the ocean like milk foam in a cup of cappuccino. Then, in a shy corner, we see a blue wave that leaves a white mark on the sand. Shortly after, a typical Californian picture reveals itself in front of us. We see a girl in a wetsuit surfing in a beautiful cove carved by the waves in the shape of a scene custom made just for her. She lies down on her belly on the surfboard and stands up every time a bigger wave appears from under the fog.

My mumbling becomes more and more articulate and lively as the bays reveal their nakedness, and the fog makes room for the landscape to express itself. We are now in Hearst San Simeon State Park, and California is showing its richness. On the side of the road, a herd of mule deer grazes with the ocean in the backdrop. Just below, at Piedras Blancas, an entire community of elephant seals rest wrapped in the cold sand. Males with elephant-like trunks and females without one swim here twice a year to rest after about ten months of aquatic life. We look at them from a railed wooden boardwalk raised above and along the beach to provide enough privacy to the seal colony. The Friends of The Elephant Seals information panels read that if the seals feel threatened in any way, they look for another refuge and won't return to these shores during the breeding and molting periods.

This is where we decide to make our way back, and that turns out to be a brilliant choice, as all the bays that hid from us on our way here, have now uncovered themselves for us without false modesty.

First stop is the famous Bixby Creek Bridge with its impressive split between two rocky hills, right on the Pacific Coast near Big Sur. We watch the fog melt into the sea, leaving behind lumps of cotton candy, among which we distinguish the backs of a few dolphins that sew the surface of the water with silver thread. I can finally fill my eyes with a clear picture of the sea. Not only. And not for long. To my complete delight, a brother and a sister, both under five, are looking in the direction of the bridge, each licking a huge multicolored lollipop. The girl licks the lollipop starting from her forearm.

We then head to McWay Falls, a waterfall that streams artistically on the beach and then into the ocean, but we manage to descend only to the middle of the trail, where a fence blocks the access due to landslides. The fog is still king in this gulf adored by photographers. Some tourists were lucky to see it clearly, as in a Windows screensaver. We see it as in a sauna.

There are about twenty people down here, and we all lean on

the wooden railing, squinting and focusing on where a pictur-esque waterfall should flow. It is there, yes, we hear it and see it for fractions of a second, stained by sticky fog. We take pictures in the waterfall's direction, but only we know that there is such a thing among the saved pixels.

Ever since M. told me we were going to Big Sur, I have wanted to visit The Henry Miller Memorial Library almost as much as the ocean. This is how the day makes up for the excessive fog ruining my expectations. Henry Miller[16] was one of my favor-ite writers in my early youth, a little below Mircea Eliade[17] and John Fowles, a little above Oscar Wilde[18], at the same level as Anais Nïn[19].

The place is charming, and I would stay here all day and come back again tomorrow. The library itself comprises a cottage of up to 500 square feet, crammed with all the books written by and about Miller. Paintings, photographs, caricatures of the writer, film adaptations posters (my favorite is Henry and June), theatre play programs, objects that had belonged to him, and framed letters cover all the walls. A treasure.

The building has a generous garden with modest mix matched tables and chairs where fans of Henry's read, write, or look into the distant fog where the ocean should be visible. I would love to sit here with them too and maybe even talk to them, just for Miller's sake. On the side of the building, on a small table, sits a full, steaming coffee maker. In front of the machine, a card lists the coffee donors, and invites visitors to help themselves to a cup, free of charge. Next to it, a box invites you to donate as much as you think is appropriate for the coffee cup. Donors and volunteers maintain the entire establishment, and they deserve all the admiration. I am leaving here with my heart swollen like a helium balloon with a postcard and a copy of Miller's first novel, Crazy Cook. And no coffee.

We continue in tandem with the ocean and the fog, passing campgrounds and a variety of hotels, restaurants with flowery terraces, RV parking lots, and gated residential communities. I noticed on the side of the road some signs that read *"Your tax *dollars at work,"* where the road had been rebuilt following land-slides.

As the sun rises from behind the hills on the right, the vegetation catches my eye. I keep asking M. to stop the car so I can see it more closely. A soft carpet of green moss dotted with purple, white, red, yellow, and orange flowers cover the cliffs that descend to the beaches and the hills that rise to the right of the road. I would roll down the valley over them, all the way down into the invisible waves. However, I refrain, with restless toes. I am ready to kick off my shoes and finally feel the sand under my feet.

Only at Garrapata Creek, a state park where the river of the same name flows into the ocean under the bridge of the same name through a spectacular rocky corridor, I finally have my chance to meet the Pacific Ocean. We take off our sneakers, roll up our pants, and take a walk to the wet and unexpectedly cold shore. The waves sweep my feet; the sand deepens under my soles; the air is salty and foggy, and I inhale it solemnly.

Upstream we cross its thin freshwater torrent several times. Ocean waves that roll up the hill against the brook splash us up to the waist covering our legs in a sweet-salty cocktail. We laugh, we chirp, we are two children looking for their childhood in the sandy waters.

Very close by, an elderly couple silently gazes at the ocean. At one point, the husband turns to his wife and kisses her on the mouth. Startled by the unexpected gesture, she scolds him, barely holding back her laughter.

*"Not in public, John. People can see us..."* I imagine her saying, her cheeks flushing with love for him. The scene is so much more adorable considering that it is just us two as the people relatively close by.

We change our clothes and drive to Point Lobos State Reserve, and then we take 17-MileDrive both engulfed in fog. We take a short break to watch the sea lions gathered in a bay near Point Pinos Lighthouse in Monterey County and a longer break in Lovers Point Park & Beach. The place is lively despite the unfortunately frowning weather. Dozens of squirrels jump like ping-pong balls from an overturned basket. Dozens of overfed ones, as chubby as a rabbit, are clearly unable to do squirrel-like acrobatic jumps like their slender siblings. (This is the perfect example as to why humans should not interfere with the wildlife feeding habits.) Children in wetsuits dive into the water from a tall pontoon, and dozens of tourists walk on the seafront with vacation sparkling in their eyes.

We stopped for lunch downtown at Hula's Island Grill. Monterey is not as picturesque as I remembered it from *Big Little Lies*. The sidewalks are like a public toilet for flocks of overweight seagulls. This doesn't stop me from enjoying a large Margarita, but it also doesn't convince me to visit more of the city.

We descend on a few more places from M.'s spreadsheet before calling it a day. Laguna Creek Beach is another place where we have no chance of swimming. But we are lucky to see a beautiful specimen of savannah cat wandering through the bushes on the coastal railroad. We admire Shark's Fin Cove from a distance, a rock that rises from the ocean just like a shark's fin. Then, we buy a growler of beer from the Highway One Brewing Company in Pescadero, which we think about intensely while visiting the Pigeon Point State Historic Park Light Station. Then, we finally enjoyed our brew in room 102 at the Comfort Inn in Half Moon Bay, California.

# 30 - *SAN FRANCISCO, BLACK SAND BEACH, BICENTENNIAL CAMPGROUND, CA*

L ess than an hour further north, the famous city of San Francisco greets us, at mile 7,878. We spend the day in the city until late afternoon, visiting as much as we can, squeezing through an unimaginable crowd of tourists.

We start with the classics - the 16th Street Painted Stairs, Lombard Street, Coit Tower, Painted Ladies, and Yerba Buena Island. We also spot from afar the island of Alcatraz with the famous prison on top, like a two-tier cake. We can't miss a cable car ride, therefore take a round trip from downtown to Fisherman's Wharf and back. Lastly, we eat a delicious lunch for dinner at the Pacific Catch. Overall, we have a clear, bright, and golden-Californian day, except for when we want to seal the deal with the piece de la resistance in San Fran, the Golden Gate Bridge.

We leave the city where living on a boat is cheaper than living in an apartment and we go in the direction of Sausalito, just across the Golden Gate Bridge. We cannot spot the bridge until we are driving on it, and we can only distinguish suspended pieces of it, not the whole thing. A shroud of opaque fog envelops the entire complex and spectacular structure. It measures almost 8,981 feet in length and just turned eighty last year. Thankfully, we still have a chance to see it in its entirety from the campsite where we will spend the night. Four months ago, we reserved a tent spot for this specific reason.

Before setting up the tent, we treat ourselves to an exotic stop at Black Sand Beach in Golden Gate National Recreation Area. A rather long and steep slope takes us from the parking lot to the beach, but incomparably easier than the trails we have hiked so far on this trip.

*"It's nice until you have to go back up!"* says a guy smiling and panting as we cross paths.

He's bare-chested, barely breathing, and his skin exhibits a bright red tone. He probably went for a swim in the cold water.

His girlfriend doesn't say anything, maybe because it's hard for her to talk and walk at the same time. I am familiar with that shortcoming. We smile back and encourage them as they are nearing the parking lot.

The beach looks deserted at first, but as we walk along the shore, we notice some commotion at the end of the bay. We are witnessing a *trash the dress*[20] scene in which a newlywed couple and a photographer are involved in a remote photo shoot. His tuxedo, her wedding dress, and their slender silhouettes move obediently to the photographer's instructions. I think it was a great idea choosing this place for their after-wedding photos. The sand looks like poppy seeds, the waves like milk foam; the contrast makes the sand blacker and the sea foam whiter. These details will be highly appreciated in the framed picture they will later place on the mantle for everyone to see.

Bicentennial Campground is different from the others we have stayed at so far and much smaller. Extremely small. M. told me that he caught the last spot when he made the reservation. Now, I understand why. There are three campsites available in total. In one of the spots, a father and his daughter are playing cards at the picnic table. An army green tent stays erected in the vicinity. The other two places are empty for now. Since we don't see the exact numbering system anywhere, we investigate where to set up our tent. Our goal is to be as close as possible to the un-fenced view of the Golden Gate Bridge (which, by the way, is red).

Our reservation reads space No. 2, but it is on the first-come-first-served basis. So, we set up our tent on the spot closest to the bridge in question, which is still not visible due to the fog, but we are optimistic for tomorrow morning.

As we settle in and take our tent lamps, beers, and snacks out on the picnic table for a pre-bedtime review-of-the-day talk, M. notices identifying numbers hanging from the grills next to each camping pitch. We seem to be currently occupying spot No. 3. We contemplate whether to move or not, because maybe the others will come after nightfall. Maybe they will not see the numbers and will set up their tent in the only free space. After further investigations, M. notices that the same paper with the spot number also states the names of the people who made the reservation and the check-in and checkout dates. It looks like this spot was already booked since last night for three days.

Elegantly and well-balanced, we move our already set tent from one place to another, under the critical eyes of the father at No. 1, who probably took this opportunity to teach his daughter a valuable lesson about life:

*"You see, my child, this is what happens when you only care about yourself and don't respect the rules. You have to move your-already-set-up-tent in the middle of the night like a crazy person! Look at those two. They thought that they could get away with taking some-one else's place, but they got caught. Don't ever do that, dear."*

Fifteen minutes after the funny and elegantly performed scene and with no qualms of conscience, a couple comes on the scene. With their hiking boots and backpacks go straight to spot No. 3 and start unpacking and setting up their tent. Looks like we have thus avoided an embarrassing situation in which the daughter of the father at No. 1 would have had a little live demonstration of her father's earlier teachings.

# 31 - *FORT BRAGG, GLASS BEACH, DRIVE-THROUGH-TREE - LEGGETT, LIVING CHIMNEY TREE - PHILLIPSVILLE, AVENUE OF THE GIANTS, HUMBOLDT, ARCATA, CA*

T his doesn't resemble an enchanting morning somewhere on a Florida beach in the Gulf of Mexico. Here, on the Californian Pacific Coast, it is cold, windy, and foggy in the middle of summer. The Golden Gate Bridge remains elusive for the time being in this morning's equation. We spot wild rabbits, birds with sharp tufts on the tops of their heads, and a deer with barely sprouted horns on the path that leads us to Point Bonita Lighthouse.

The lighthouse keeps its distance, as it is closed for business, but the walk to and from gets our blood pumping. On the way back, we see hundreds of harbor seals stretched out like a carpet on a bulging rock near the water. According to the information panel along the trail, they come from afar to rest and spend quality time here with their pups.

Having failed to see the bridge already twice we make peace with this loss and carry on with our journey, keeping the ocean to the left. The road sews the dense and rich forests on the right to the pretentious shore. The car thermometer shows the outside temperature rising whenever the road goes deep into the woods, away from the ocean, and it lowers whenever we drive in parallel with the fog-wrapped shore again. There are serene skies over the forest and low visibility over the shore.

On the side of the road, hundreds of cyclists go up and down in small or large groups lined up at the curb, and take breaks in the charming towns along the shoreline. Dozens of Ferraris and Porsches in bright colors drive in the opposite direction. Motorcyclists pass us, and we pass RVs. We pass nomadic cyclists with bulky luggage placed like sacks on the back of a donkey. M. tells me that they start from the Canadian border and stop at the Mexican border or vice versa. Respect!

Quite often, we find cars that tow motorboats, and in areas where the ocean creates huge bays, we see them launching those boats into the water. The traffic is motley, and we already have a consistent list of man-made vehicles speeding on the coast. Submarines and helicopters are missing though, but planes surely fly high above us, hiding over the thicket of tall forests.

The area is incredibly rich and lively. We pass wild turkeys, flocks of sheep, herds of black-white-brown cows, and lonely horses grazing in the shade. The coastal towns and resorts are architectural jewels, some of which make me think of dollhouses. In front of a fire department, the trees are styled as if by Edward Scissorhands[21]. In a curve, a pine tree about ten feet high, adorned with decorations and shiny tinsel, militates for a never-ending Christmas.

Cars with license plates from all over the US and Canadian provinces smoothly populate the road. Interestingly enough, on two-way roads, if a driver notices a car behind whose driver shows impatience to pass and has no way of doing so because of the continuous double dividing line or curves, he purposely gets out of the way by pulling over on the next passing place. Signs with *"Slow traffic must use turn-out"* encourage this practice every few miles, and people do just that. Admirable!

In Fort Bragg, we take a lunch break at Silvers at the Wharf, a restaurant that, in addition to serving fresh and delicious seafood, has unrestricted views of the Noyo River flowing into the ocean. The already memorable experience becomes exceptional when two dolphins take their afternoon swim right in front of the restaurant patio.

We are getting closer to the redwood forests, the tallest trees in the world. Before we lose ourselves among them, with our heads tilted back, we make a stop at Glass Beach in MacKerricher State Park. Its unusual story made us curious. This bay, which is now crowded with tourists, and two more bays in Fort Bragg, California, were landfills for several decades since 1900. When the first one had filled up, the locals started throwing garbage in the second one and so on. Then, in the 1960s, someone woke up to reality, admitted the damage, and started rolling an ecological movement up the hill.

Biodegradable waste biodegraded over time; metal scraps from furniture, cars, or appliances were removed from beaches; and glass and ceramics shards became one with the sand, somehow fitting into the bay's anatomy. It remained like this up until today. There may be enough glass sand left for another decade, according to the amount visible to the naked eye, and at the rate hundreds of visitors sample from it daily.

We continue advancing on the map and after entering Mendocino County, advertisements for a certain Drive-Through-Tree lure us along the side of the road once every few miles. This might be the one Bill Bryson thought he had missed back in '89. We cannot resist the natural urge to drive through a tree, as it happens to many people when passing a Drive-Through-KFC or Drive-Through-Starbucks.

Not wanting to resist the attraction, in Leggett we turn right and enter an enchanted forest of redwood trees. The route is cleverly designed in the form of a loop car trail. We reach the central element of the park on one side and exit on the other. The traffic resembles a river of cars making a picturesque loop before returning to the highway. We go through the tree in slow motion and take pictures in front of it with and without a car, while the queue gets busier behind us.

Apart from the Chandelier Tree, the forest has something we have never seen before. From place to place, the stumps of thunderstruck or fallen trees are carved into animal and bird shapes, which we find creative and unique. We soon realize this is just the beginning, and that we have arrived in the homeland of wooden sculptures.

Entering the Avenue of the Giants, another enchanted tree catches our attention with signs that arouse our curiosity once again. We are not strong enough to turn it down. In Phillipsville, a redwood named the Living Chimney Tree is alive and still standing. The tree survived a fire that burned its entire interior 104 years ago, sparing its bark and roots. It seems that this is enough for the *"chimney tree"* to live peacefully and attract hundreds of tourists every day.

The owners arranged the entrance to the tree through a massive wooden door. A few steps lead to the circular room of the trunk with a diameter of twelve and a half feet at the base. Looking up, the sky greets you at the end of the vertical tunnel. Next to the tree, there is probably the only restaurant in Phillipsville, a town with a population of 140 people. They call it Chimney Tree Grill, of course. At the entrance, in front of the stairs, stands a tree trunk carved into the shape of a bear with a slightly tormented smile on its face. It's wearing overalls and a hat and is holding a growler on one shoulder.

One more step and we are on the Avenue of the Giants, a portion of State Route 254 that passes through the gorgeous Humboldt Redwoods State Park. We look tiny compared to the 230-foot-tall trees, and the car looks like a toy sliding between their endless stilts. This giant boulevard is just a preamble to what we will see tomorrow in Redwood National Park, where the tallest tree is 375 feet tall. It is named accordingly: Hyperion.

We pull over whenever we find refuge and try to capture the huge proportions of the forest in our pictures, photographing it upward from the asphalt level to fit in the frame. We also turn off the air conditioning and open the sunroof to inhale the clean scented air. I lean my head back on the headrest and gaze into the heterogeneous green canopy dotted by the blue sky.

After having driven almost 300 miles today, we arrived in Arcata, California at mile 8,243. We park on an alley behind the Arcata Hotel, downtown, next to the central park, the library, and a few homeless people. When M. chose this place for the night of July 21, 2018, he thought of offering me a different experience, booking a room in an old hotel, located in a historic building, where the owners tried to preserve the decor and the air since its inauguration in 1915.

Entering the lobby and then room 216, I can appreciate the intention and applaud it, but I cannot help feeling that I have entered a horror movie set. The mahogany vintage furniture, the dim light, the dark green cast iron radiator, the wallpaper, the blanket and the busy pattern curtains, the bathroom with a freestanding claw foot tub, and the shower curtain make me think of a bloody crime set. While M. is gone to do laundry, I take a shower. I keep looking at the bathroom door from behind the curtain and through the mirror, just to make sure a killer will not sneak in. I hold my breath as I tiptoe my way out of the bathroom, look discreetly into the room, and run aiming for the phone to call M. and ask him to come back quickly. I can't handle this level of suspense by myself. He left his phone on the bed, and my heart is pounding when I hear the ringtone. This is the vibe of the room by and large. My imagination is a bit rich, I admit, considering that I never watch horror movies.

The night passes in slow motion. All the noises startle me. I fall asleep late, exhausted after listening for hours to the furniture creaking with old age, the other doors in the hotel squeaking, and noisy groups of young people partying right under our window, laughing grotesquely and smashing beer bottles on the curb.

# 32 - *REDWOOD NATIONAL PARK, MILL CREEK CAMPGROUND, DEL NORTE REDWOOD STATE PARK, CA*

I t's Sunday morning. I wake up already tired but happy that I survived my imagination, and that I am alive. I can't leave here fast enough and hopefully I'll never have to return. M. is fresh and cheerful and has no idea about the movie I played all night in my head. I realize how silly I would seem so I don't even mention it to him.

Breakfast at the Big Blue Café brings me back to earth and back to a relaxed holiday. The venue is full of locals with children running around and babies prattling in infant carriers. We are witnessing an American custom that I already love. Sunday breakfast. Everywhere in this vast country, Sunday's breakfast is family time at the diner. Bill Bryson knew it well and wrote about it in his book *The Lost Continent – Travels in small-town America*. *"Everybody in America goes out for Sunday breakfast. It is such a popular pastime that you generally have to line up for a table, but it's always worth the wait."*

We spent our last day on the California Pacific Coast in Redwood National Park in a blockbuster movie setting. As usual, we choose a few trails in different directions of the park to taste as much as possible of the specifics of the place. We trust the first lady of the '63-'69 America, the wife of President Lyndon B. Johnson, who succeeded John F. Kennedy. They named the trail after her because of her involvement in protecting this park. Her dedication to nature expanded nationwide, and one of her outstanding actions was to beautify urban areas.

Lady Bird Johnson Grove is a forest descended from fairy tales, and the walk along the circular path takes us completely out of everyday life and off the map. We meander through a botanical atlas. Among the redwood giants that fill the whole picture are clovers, ferns, redwood sorrel, and berries that stretch like a living carpet in all directions. We look at this seemingly invincible and immortal forest, but its history was written by decades of the massive deforestation that only ceased in the late 1960s. By then, 90% of the original forest had been cut down. Thanks to the people who saw beyond the raw material and understood the ecological richness of these places, the forest is still a paradise of fauna and flora that can only thrive here.

A few miles further north we enter the Trillium Falls trail. We just can't say no to waterfalls. At the end of the path, right at the foot of the bridge, in front of the waterfall, a 100-year-old woman reads a book sitting in a folding chair with hiking poles and a backpack next to it. Honestly, the woman is more exotic than the waterfall. I love people who read in public!

Ten miles up the coast, in Prairie Creek Redwoods State Park, we stop to present ourselves to Fern Canyon, an impressive tourist attraction, thanks to the notoriety of *The Lost World: Jurassic Park* and the dinosaurs from the BBC documentaries. After only a few tens of steps inside the steep valley, we fully understand why Spielberg brought his cameras here. Soft moss and ferns of five different varieties, in different stages of growth, line the green universe between the fifty-foot-tall walls of the canyon. The Home Creek plays hide and seek among bushy or delicate ferns and looks fragile among boulders or under log bridges. The setting is heavenly, like a terrarium arranged with care by nature on a much larger scale.

We leave this place whispering with the sound of ferns still rustling in our ears. We pass by campgrounds nestled on the shores of the ocean and past meadows where groups of elk graze quietly, aware of the extinction of the dinosaurs. Then, for tens of miles, we look for a place to eat lunch. All we find are souvenir shops where the most popular products are Bigfoot wooden sculptures.

Not until Klamath do we manage to find a cooked meal. At Forest Cafe the food is 99% deep-fried. Groups of tourists gathered from probably a twenty-mile radius overcrowd the place, but the decor washes away all its sins. Decorative duck bellies and feet hang from the ceiling as if we were on the bottom of a lake looking up seeing wild ducks swimming above.

We have been on the Pacific Coast for a few days now, and I can no longer tolerate not being able to get a tan. It seems to be sunnier today, so I tell M. to look for the nearest beach on the map. In ten minutes, we are lying down on a towel in the sun in False Klamath Cove. M. is fully dressed like everyone else, and I am in a bathing suit. I stand still, to feel the heat of the sun on my skin as intensely as possible. Through intense meditation, I manage to ignore the wind that freezes my nose, fingers, and toes. It is a necessary experience for me, but difficult, having to juggle with the body heat and the cooler climate. Now, I can say that I went to the beach at the Pacific Ocean, and by doing so, checked off from the list the only complaint.

We will spend the night in Del Norte Redwood State Park in Mill Creek Campground. We make it there before nightfall. We set up the tent on spot No. 123, while a chipmunk eats a snack sitting in perfect balance on a vigorous fern leaf, right next to the picnic table. The campground is full to the brim, and the noise that rises above the tents and RVs makes me feel like it's summer vacation back in elementary school. If I prick up my ears, I catch snippets of conversation from the neighbors next door. According to their voices, they seem to be around fifty years old, and their stories revolve around the trips they had taken back in the day with the same gang and the adventures they had had together. They laugh loudly and toast plastic cups, and I listen to them thinking of my parents and their friends and the jokes they said around the fire by our old blue tent when vacationing across Romania.

Then, I go to wash up, and the restroom offers me a new first-experience with its pay showers. I go back to the tent to warn M. Then, take some coins and return to the facility. As I stand in front of the instruction panel of the shower, a woman sees me puzzled and begins to explain exactly what I have to do:

*"Oh honey, never used this kind of shower before, have you? Here's what you gotta do: you put in four quarters and that will last you seven minutes of water. If you need more time, just add more quarters."*

This is how they do it in campgrounds in this country. People are kind and want to help, and water is used wisely. These two things made my vacation even more beautiful - people and their respect for nature. When I return to the tent, I see a ranger woman taking a tour of the campground, asking people if everything is fine and wishing them a good night. Yes, such a thing does exist, although it exceeds any expectations I could have had from a simple tent experience. They have all my respect!

# CHAPTER VIII - *OREGON, THE BEAVER STATE*

# 33 - *ARCH ROCK VIEW POINT, SISTERS ROCK STATE PARK, HECETA HEAD LIGHTHOUSE, NEPTUNE STATE SCENIC VIEWPOINT, CAPE PERPETUA, SIUSLAW NATIONAL FOREST, CA ☼ CANNON BEACH, OR ☼ LONG BEACH, WA*

A t mile 8,372, we enter the Oregon coast. The Beaver State. The ocean is still to our left, but here the fog covers it even more fiercely if that were possible. And it is! We head north until we reach the northernmost point of the continental states in Cape Flattery.

The road is almost deserted and at the first two stops, at Arch Rock View Point and Sisters Rock State Park, it is just the two of us on the shore. It is still very early. On top of that, it is Monday morning. So, this might have to do with why we are the only ones looking at the shapeless beaches and the rocks emerging from the water and fog like giant marine animal heads this time of day.

My stomach makes hungry animal sounds, because here, on the coast highway, you don't just stumble upon Walmart or Target. That is why we did not have a place to stock up for the night in a campground. However, we are confident that we will find an eatery and a cooked breakfast this Monday morning. We do find one indeed, only two hours after leaving the campsite, when the morning hunger combines with the lunch hunger and turns me into an unbearable co-pilot. I'm about to refuse to visit anything else until I feel at least an omelet mixing with coffee in my belly, when we notice on the side of the road a sturdy shack, with a *Greasy Spoon Café* sign on the roof.

We slow down to see if it is open, and I already feel more lively noticing happy and satiated people sitting at the tables on the patio stroking their bellies with satisfaction. We hit the brakes, park the car, and then everything becomes a poem in which omelets, bacon, tomatoes, avocado, cheese, toast, and hot coffee rhyme in gastronomic verses.

I am a whole human again. I regain the joy that usually characterizes me, and this way M. unknowingly avoids encountering a disgraceful R. Once again, bacon saves me! With hunger off the radar, the day looks friendlier and the sun more benevolent over the ocean fog. The vegetation on the Oregon coast is as rich and dense as in California, but many more wildflowers embellish the area. Countless front yard flower beds give the villages we pass through a pastoral ikebana vibe.

We stop at Heceta Head Lighthouse and manage to see the entire building, roof and all, which far exceeds our expectations because of the fog. At Neptune Beach, our wishes go unfulfilled again with the unpredictable fog following us around. The Cummins Creek flows into the ocean digging a canal along the cobbled beach, after a slim limbo demonstration under the bridge of the same name. We manage to see almost three-quarters of the artistic-engineering structure of the bridge arch, and we say thank you for having been so lucky. The fog keeps the score and is always one foot ahead of us.

What comes next is a masculine extravagance of a wild and rocky landscape in which the ocean seems to be at war with the shore in an endless winnerless battle. Each has only one weapon at its disposal, water versus stone, and the weather is an ally that changes sides depending on the wind. We are in Cape Perpetua, part of the Siuslaw National Forest. The beach and the bay resemble a vast battlefield on the face of which the battles between terrestrial and extraterrestrial deities have left a deep imprint. The rocky shore looks like a minefield after all the bombs have been stepped on. White foam and black rocks fiercely jump at each other's throats with every wave.

The list of fierce names continues here with Devil's Churn, a narrow, long channel carved into the forty million year-old lava foreshore, which fills up with each torrent. When two waves overlap, the water hits the edges in a cold and noisy explosion. At Cook's Chasm, I lose M., because it is quite far from the safe shore. If you want to get as close to it as possible, you risk the water splashing you, gushing from all the cracks it dug through the basalt rocks. I stand quietly and watch the whole expanse of water-invaded foreshore while M. is in the trenches, watching closely as the water breaks loose through The Spouting Horn and flows back into the ocean through Thor's Well as if through a funnel. It's difficult for me to separate M. from Cape Perpetua and carry on to another destination named after the devil. For days on end afterwards, we keep talking about how the water burst out of The Spouting Horn. Pressure, volume, speed, and sound. Sheer physics.

In another hour, we reach the Devil's Punch Bowl Arch, where a cup-shaped rock fills up with water through a small arch, constantly emptying and filling up again. The ocean gives the impression of a determined waiter who depends on Mr. Devil's gratuity, in exchange for always keeping its glass full.

The Pacific Coast is crammed with the most fantastic rock formations and they all have names that artistically reflect reality. The same happens at Cannon Beach, where Haystack Rock sits on the shore in the identical shape of (obviously) a haystack.

Arriving here, my stomach reminds me that it has been about seven hours since I've last eaten. As we find ourselves in the midst of a full-on seaside resort, we walk along the coast in search of lunch or dinner. In America, the menus are different for each meal of the day. So, at breakfast, you can't order lunch and at dinner, you can't ask for breakfast. For us, this has never been a problem, because around 4 or 5 pm we usually eat linner[22].

However, here in Cannon Beach, we can't seem to find availability in any of the restaurants we enter, as we must have made a reservation in advance. That is what they tell us. Hunger forces us to try our luck on the crowded streets in search of an available table, even if we have to share it with someone else. Luckily, we found two empty seats at the bar in Bill's Tavern & Brewhouse. As usual, we ask for the catch of the day, as one should do when in waterfront restaurants, where they cook freshly caught fish every morning directly from the anglers. Here, the halibut is the catch of the day and from now on, it is my favorite fish dish.

Oregon remains behind and Washington, the Evergreen State replaces it under the wheels of our car. Starting from California upwards, I notice that the fog is ever-present on the coast and increases in opacity as we advance. After driving about 375 miles, we spent the night in Long Beach, another beautiful seaside resort, where we reached 8,732 miles. We enter the city as the night is falling, foggy, and lightly drizzling. The streets are deserted, but you can see that the hotels and restaurants are full of tourists who apparently want to spend the summer in a land of cold and fog. Wet and cold weather is no exception to these parts but the rule.

Room 11 at the Coastal Inn is the chicest so far. The bedding and paintings have a marine theme in shades of blue and light cream; a wicker lampshade rests on a navy porcelain base; the furniture is all white; soft plush white robes await us behind the bathroom door; and the bed is so comfortable that I feel weightless.

# CHAPTER IX -

## *WASHINGTON, THE EVERGREEN STATE*

# 34 - *KALALOCH TREE ROOT CAVE AND BEACH, RUBY BEACH, RIALTO BEACH, HALL OF MOSSES - OLYMPIC NATIONAL PARK, CAPE FLATTERY, BONNEY LAKE, WA*

We draw the curtains, and the room is flooded with strong morning sunlight that we have been missing for at least a week. It is the last day on the Pacific Coast, and it promises to be glorious. We have ahead of us a nine-hour drive to Seattle, with a considerable detour through the upper left corner of the map of the United States of America, from where, on such a clear day, we should be able to see the Canadian coast.

We head slightly upwards, parallel to the ocean, drawing unequal zigzags between the shore and the mainland. We passed through green areas with rich vegetation, through Quinault Rain Forest, and then through Olympic National Park, where they filmed the Twilight series. We aren't fans, so we're not curious to visit the town of Forks and the surroundings inhabited by fictional vampires.

Instead, we stop to see Kalaloch Tree Root Cave and Beach, a little further south than Forks, where a Sitka spruce, the largest of the spruce kind, retains its verticality although it is not stuck in the ground, like most trees. If not all. *The Tree of Life* or *The Runaway Tree*, as they also call it, stands with its roots split above the high and steep bank. From under it, the ground slipped due to a stream that flows underneath and then flows into the ocean. The water carried the earth beneath it, little by little, until the spruce roots remained bare, like the branches above. Below, it formed an entrance that is maybe ten feet high and fifteen feet wide, which perfectly resembles a cave. The tree rests on its peripheral roots, which seem long but fragile. Some people come daily to make sure it hasn't collapsed yet, that's how unlikely its balance is.

It seems that around these places the sun has almost run out of light and heat for today. We adjust again to the fog, wind, and more recently, the clouds that darken considerably the ambience on Ruby Beach.

The novelty that meets us on the beaches of Washington (and we have not met so far on the coast of the southern states) is the shocking amount of driftwood lying along the shore. The rivers that flow into the ocean bring dry trunks from the upper forests and throw them on the beaches in huge stacks. On Rialto Beach, we find even more driftwood, and see dozens of people gathering small pieces of it, probably for sculptures or jewelry.

Going deeper into the continent, we find the twin brother of the dark sun from the coast, shining hot through the Hoh Rain Forest, making the green of the forest shine emerald. We visit the Hall of Mosses, an exceptional part of Olympic National Park, where green and brown velvet completely wrap the maples and spruce trees. Due to the proximity of the ocean, high mountains, and heavy rains, this rainforest ignores the geographical boundaries that place it so far from the tropics and appropriate their lush richness. The trees, entirely covered in thick moss that flows from the branches to the ground, make me think of an enchanted forest in which personified trees play in nature's self-sufficient theater.

We head to Cape Flattery, the Land of the Makah Tribe, and the most northwestern point in the contiguous United States. This is also the spot where our journey will change its course and will start heading east. It will inevitably close the circle (or whatever geometrical shape our trip has managed to design) we began in Illinois. Another week and the story of this adventure will have its final form. It will be the compact memory of an exceptional summer.

This corner of the world is not easy to cross. Not because of the infrastructure, but because of the contrast it makes to the rest of the Pacific Coast. The poor fishing villages of the Makah tribe replace the towns we passed through a week ago, with chic cottages, front yard flower beds, crowded restaurants, and streets full of tourists. It looks like the Romanian countryside, but the yards here have no fences and are all neat. Except for a pickup truck or a boat, there is nothing else in the front yards.

Cape Flattery welcomes us with the usual cold, wind, fog, and clouds, but without rain, which allows us to reach the cliff from where we should see Vancouver Island. Of course, it's not to be seen, but the trail to and from the parking lot is a whispered poem. The boardwalk meanders like a pontoon among the tall conifers. Towards the end, the terrain narrows. Left and right, we see the precipice coast with all shapes of sea stacks that spring out of the ocean and push the fog with flat, forested peaks. Right at the end of the hike, a tree with its branches contorted by the harsh wind, acts as a prop that appears in most pictures taken by tourists.

The ocean has dug into the stone shore bays and created moss covered caves with smooth edges. I refuse to imagine what the landscape would look like if instead of fog and clouds there was only the sun alone above. I hold on to the hope that another time in my life I will return here and find the ocean and the forest in pigmented colors and the horizon revealed below a clear sky.

Until then, we say goodbye to the Pacific Ocean and head east to Seattle. A dear friend I haven't seen in about seventeen years is waiting for us with her husband and cat. She must have already started dinner for us.

A few tens of miles before Seattle, words are stuck in my throat as Mount Rainier appears in front of us at the end of the highway. I rub my eyes just like a cartoon character and then blink as if a mosquito was stuck under my eyelids. I ask questions as if no answer could really match my amazement:

*"M., what is that in the distance? What is going on there?"*

It is a mountain, I see it well, but it seems so close, big, and impossible to be real. As everything around is flat, and at sea level, the mountain rises out of nowhere. Unfathomable. Its apparition charms me, and I can't look anywhere else. My eyes are glued to the windshield.

At mile 9,210, we park in front of my friend's house, extremely happy to see each other again and greet noisily. I am surprised by the resilience of this relationship that has survived since childhood and deeply impressed by how little we have changed in all this time.

Our hunger is the size of the chicken, potatoes and asparagus casserole cooking in the oven, and the appetite for storytelling matches the bottles of wine that flood the evening with memories from another life.

# 35 - *SEATTLE, WA*

We spent Wednesday in Seattle, starting with breakfast on the back patio. My friend is immune to the view and doesn't even notice it anymore, just like the Sacramento couple from Arches. Mount Rainier mesmerizes us, standing straight and conic, as if on top of the neighboring houses' roofs. I might think of Seattle as the city where one can see Mount Rainier, and it would be enough to win my eternal admiration.

Before returning to the patio in the evening, we make a few stops: the famous Fish Market, a kind of circus where the fish are acrobats; Kerry Park from where we can see the city's skyline down below; and Gasworks Park where we rest our eyes on Union Lake dotted with yachts and sailboats. Then, we visited the Art Museum in front of which one of the twelve Hammering Men industrial art sculptures knock tirelessly in honor of workers around the world. Similar sculptures are set up across the United States, Europe, and Asia.

We take an elegant lunch break on the deck at Chandler's Crabhouse, where I devour a few crabs - Dungeness, Alaskan King, and Bairdi, smearing myself with butter and spices up to my elbows. We spent the evening on the patio at my friend's house with the full moon discreetly illuminating the snowy peak of the volcano.

# 36 - *RAINIER NATIONAL PARK, NARADA FALLS, REFLECTION LAKE, BOX CANYON, YAKIMA, WA*

On Thursday, we set off in a group of four to Rainier National Park, which has its foothill sewn tightly by hundreds of cyclists who ride a marathon that looks more like an ordeal. We manage to pass them without any accidents, but for this performance to be successful, we over abuse the horn. Most of them pull to the right side of the road, but some of them seem to lose their balance from all the exhaustion. Maybe their feet just lose grip of the paddles, or they temporarily lose their focus because they end up in the middle of the lane.

We park near the Dead Horse Creek Trailhead, at the end of which the Glacier Point Overlook awaits us. Theoretically, we will be able to have a snowball fight, and from there, we will descend to Henry M. Jackson Memorial Visitor Center.

We choose this trail because on paper it seems easy. About two-three miles, half ascent and half descent. We don't want to exhaust our friends who say that they haven't climbed the mountain in the last eight years or so. My friend is neither equipped for what we are going to do nor aware of the effort it will take to climb. However, she is extremely happy that we are together, and I hope that the enthusiasm will propel her at least halfway through. Her husband is ecstatic, because he had spent his adolescence and the first part of his youth on these trails. Then, for years, he just looked at the mountain from their back patio, somewhat nostalgic that his wife didn't share his passion. Now, they are both here because of us.

She doesn't talk much, trying to control her breathing as well as possible, and when she decides to participate in the conversation, she only snaps jokingly at M.

*"I will kill you! Why did you bring me here?!"* She laughs and makes fun of the once athletic body of hers, which now does not help her much uphill. Her husband is so happy to be here again that he does not even notice that the soles of his boots shatter

with each step, leaving behind traces of dried rubber crumbs. They dry rotted! He had kept them in the basement, hoping to wear them again someday, and now that their turn is up, they fall apart heroically. He returns to the car to change his shoes, and then we take it back up the hill in a queue led by M.

The sky is 200% clearer. The green of the pine forest goes through all the Pantone hues. The wildflowers are more than we have ever seen in one place and their bright colors stain the green of the grass. Chipmunks and blue jays animate this HD wallpaper view. The trail is paved and climbs steeply in wide curves to the permanent glacier at the top of the volcano.

Hundreds of tourists climb taking their time and unveil their teeth for pictures guarded by the mountain. Several groups of serious mountaineers descend from the glacier with crampons and axes tied to their backpacks. M. stops one of them to ask about crevasses, duration, and difficulty of the hike. He explains to us in incredible detail of how he will one day climb Rainier himself, which serves as a training mountain for those who want to try their luck on the mountains of Nepal.

The last part of the path that leads to an area where the patches of snow widen more and more, I climb only with M. The other couple are waiting for us somewhere on a boulder, warming in the sun. We then go down to the Visitor Center where we eat Mexican burritos and German sausages for lunch. From the gift shop, I leave with a pair of dragonfly-shaped earrings. Before we part ways, we go down together to Narada Falls, where we promise to see each other more often in the next twenty years. Then, we say goodbye and move on to Yakima.

We make a short stop at Reflection Lake where Mount Rainier's imposing figure is thrown back wrinkly by the surface of the lake due to a light breeze. It stands above the water just like a scoop of vanilla ice cream, and once again, I find it as unreal as I did two days ago. We then stop at Box Canyon, to admire it only from a distance, from a bridge that stands above the melted waters that carve their way down from the glacier.

Yakima looks deserted, as does the Days Inn hotel where we

spend the night in room 233. It may not be deserted. It probably just seems like that to us after two days spent with other people. Alternatively, I have another theory: as we are nearing the end of this American vacation, nostalgia is gradually overwhelming us. Tomorrow, we will have to drive for 500 miles. That will give us plenty of time to ponder the reality of this trip ending.

# CHAPTER X - *IDAHO, FAMOUS POTATOES* ☼ *MONTANA, BIG SKY COUNTRY*

# 37 - *PALOUSE FALLS STATE PARK, COEUR D'ALENE NATIONAL FOREST, WA ☼ FLATHEAD NATIONAL FOREST, BIGFORK, MT ☼ FISH CREEK CAMPGROUND - GLACIER NATIONAL PARK, WY*

At mile 9,380, we leave Yakima. After two and a half hours of crossing endless fields of hops and apple and cherry orchards, we stopped for a late breakfast in Palouse Falls State Park. It is still very early, and we are the first tourists to reach the waterfall. The ranger has not come yet to sign the register, so we don't have anyone to pay the state park fee.

We silently eat the breakfast my friend from Seattle packed for us and watch the waterfall from a distance. A few miles before flowing into the Snake River, the Palouse River has an artistic fall of about 200 feet in height, an extreme sport it has been performing for the last 13,000 years. More or less. It represents a source of praise for the state of Washington and a meeting spot for painters and photographers countrywide.

At mile 9,655, we enter Idaho. Tens of miles later, we exit the famous Potato State and enter Montana, Big Sky Country. After passing Spokane, Idaho, what follows is a completely new relief on the map compared to the last forty days. We cross the Coeur D'Alene National Forest and then the Flathead National Forest, woods that intertwine one into the next far over the Canadian border. It smells of pine and clean river water. Among the trunks of trees that betray a homogeneous age, there are compact and opaque forests, different from those seen so far, where young trees rise among the remains of those burned by wildfires.

It is raining lazily. This vacation has seen rain so rarely that I am only now beginning to remember the healing power of rain.

In Dayton, Montana, a small town on the shores of Lake Flathead, we pass beautiful houses built on a hill, with landscaped front yards, no fences, short cut grass, boats, and RVs in driveways, all of them facing the lake. We pass other towns with houses built deep into the forest, showing only their roofs among the foliage that poke the rain clouds. In the distance, I see the Rockies with their snow-capped peaks. Plenty of RV parks with playgrounds and large boat halls dot the area.

We leave the rain behind. On the other side of the lake, we stop in Bigfork, a mountain resort resembling a freshly finished painting by a corny artist. The streets are crowded with tourists, who are probably looking for a place to have dinner after a day of walking, fishing, sailing, cycling, or horseback riding. Many venues advertise live music and movie festivals.

The streets bordering the lake attract visitors to hotels, restaurants, cafes, gift shops, art galleries, and travel agencies. It is almost dinnertime and most of the restaurants are busy. We enter a few of them and ask for a table for two, but without a reservation, they can't serve us. And we're lucky to be turned around, because we end up having dinner sitting outside at the Bigfork Inn, the most beautiful locale around. We sit at a corner table on the deck patio from where we can catch a glimpse of the lake and the streets crammed with strolling tourists.

While waiting for the catch of the day we ordered, we orient ourselves on the map of the city and the lake printed on the paper table mat. It looks like we are only one-hour's drive away from Fish Creek Campground, where we have reserved the tent place number B49.

Since we have been bragging about how much we missed a healthy rain, we experience a good downpour right as we enter Glacier National Park. And the rain keeps at it over the campground all through the night. It pours and shows no signs of stopping. We begin setting up our temporary house with water dripping down our backs and gathering in puddles in the corners of the tent. We wipe as much of it as we can with the clothes from our backs that are already wet and then leave them outside under the cover.

We are relatively dry in the clothes and sleeping bags brought from the car under the torrent and sincerely grateful that we didn't drop them in the running mud. It takes me a very long time to fall asleep, with the roar of the water beating the drum on the waterproof tent, but what mostly keeps me awake is a strong desire to visit the gorgeous Glacier National Park under clear skies. One thing is reassuring though, this is my first time sleeping in a tent when I don't think bears would bother attacking innocent people in the middle of a downpour.

# 38 - *GLACIER NATIONAL PARK, HELENA, MT*

T he morning is cold and the moisture is penetrating the ground, the sky, and my stiff joints. The tent retained its bright orange color though, no matter how much it rained. I expected it to fade overnight. It is full of resin and mud. Since we have nowhere to stretch it to dry, we pack it with half a gallon of rainwater, at least two pounds of pine needles, and a few crushed cones from last night. We have nowhere to sit and eat breakfast, because the bench and the picnic table are wet and the trees are still shaking off the rain. We decided to eat our morning salad in the parking lot where we'll start on the first trail to Avalanche Lake.

The day slowly opens over the park with the chirping of birds and the rustling of freshly watered forests. M. is also here for the first time, so we discover everything together, and as far as we can tell, this park is gigantic. Luckily, we are used to waking up very early in the morning, because the trailhead parking lots are almost full all along the way, and we can barely find a place to eat our salad. We stand next to the car, disposable bowls in hand, and eat as we watch visitors of all ages and shapes equip themselves and head for the trails in the area.

Yesterday, when I still didn't know much about Glacier, I chose the most popular trail in the brochure for the first part of the day, the one to Avalanche Lake. It lies on the western side of the park, and we will spend the afternoon in the eastern one. I read that we could take a ferry across the lakes of Many Glacier to an area of rich wildlife.

Avalanche Lake is a glacial lake into which flow several waterfalls formed by the melting of the Sperry Glacier, which sits cold somewhere behind the peak of Little Matterhorn. The hike begins with the Trail of the Cedars, a footbridge that winds through an old cedar forest and western hemlocks, where the Avalanche brook forms spectacular gorges. After stepping off the mile and a half long boardwalk, the trail climbs along the body of water, until it reaches its source, at about 3,905 feet of altitude, where it unloads the crowds of tourists on a wide and smooth beach.

We rest on one of the log benches placed at the edge of the forest, facing the still water of the glacial lake. The view is clear after last night's rain. Bearhat Mountain, Little Matterhorn, the sky, pine trees, and waterfalls reflect together into the Avalanche Lake like into an oversized mirror. The water is so clear that the bottom of the lake seems to be just a few feet deep. Boulders and trunks drifted into the lake in this spring's thaw, you can see clearly, as if they were floating on the surface.

The silence condenses in this valley and everyone whispers. It's as if the voices could break the mirror of the water and with it the world's peace. Moreover, we gesture when an over-energetic chipmunk checks our backpack and jackets left on the bench, and we laugh silently when it starts to check all the other tourists sitting at the edge of the forest.

On the way down, we cross paths with hundreds of tourists going up to the lake, single or in groups, and once again, I think of how impressed I am to see nature-loving people. Halfway through the trek, we pass a family that fails to convince its seven or eight year-old daughter to continue. She cries and screams that she doesn't want to walk another foot. The mother tells her calmly (and I think, convincingly) that at the end of the path, they will reach a beautiful lake where they will rest and have a picnic. The little girl shouts at the top of her lungs, *"I dooooon't caaaaaaare!"* Certainly, mountain trails are not a thing of beauty for everyone or maybe not for all ages.

We hop in the car and head east, where we hope to take a ferry ride and hike a few more miles. The GPS says that in one hour we will reach the other entrance. In about eighty miles to be exact, which says a lot about the immensity of this park. In the meantime, I read aloud from the brochure we received entering the park last night, and everything we learned about it is impressive.

It covers an area of 1,583 square miles and extends beyond

the Canadian border, joining national parks in Alberta and British Columbia. Of the 700 existing lakes, 130 are notable and named, and over 200 waterfalls are visible along the park from spring to fall. Of the 150 glaciers that existed two centuries ago, only twenty-five still exist. Scientists believe that by 2030 they will completely withdraw due to global warming. Over a hundred trails dot the park and it would probably take us two to three weeks to visit the most notable. What we do today is just a drop in a bucket, but we are happy with that either way.

The area was declared a national park in 1910. The native reservations of the tribes who had been living here were preserved and still exist today - Blackfeet in the east of the park and Flathead in the east and south. The most important engineering achievement that the park needed, which was completed over a span of five years in 1932, is Going-to-the-Sun Road. The road crosses the park through the Rocky Mountains from east to west. It measures forty-nine miles and reaches 6,646 feet of altitude when driving on Logan Pass.

Going up to Many Glacier, we also have to take the Going-to-the-Sun Road and cross the Logan Pass. Caught in a row of thousands of cars moving in slow motion, we go through a grandiose landscape. We stop at every panoramic point to admire the gorgeous backdrop. What seems to be a piece of heaven is Lake St. Mary and Goose Island, barely sticking out of the water. Mountain peaks over 5,000 feet high border the lake, the most spectacular of which is Little Chief Mountain. Sequences from The Shining were filmed above the lake, and Forrest Gump was caught running on Going-to-the-Sun Road during his jogging phase.

There are no parking lots along the pass, so the road looks like a treadmill that makes short breaks at every pullout. Here too, shuttle buses are available to tourists, transporting them from one place to another. In addition to the shuttles, the Red Jammers offer guided tours. They are red vintage buses from the 1930s that have been preserved and modernized. Every time we intersect with one of them, we have the impression of going back in time about a hundred years. In front of us, there is a convertible with Illinois license plates, in which four people with funny looking hats on their heads enjoy the sun and the landscape, with the top down.

Arriving at the Many Glaciers entrance, we ran out of luck. We wait in a line that is much too long and goes much too fast to be good news. Near the gate, a ranger in a uniform, badge, and wide-brimmed hat stops each car and informs the driver that the park is full. Only those who have a ferry reservation can enter. Those who don't are politely asked to return, either later in the evening or another day but much earlier in the morning. Around 10 am, this area of the park reaches the maximum number of visitors, and they don't allow overcrowding. Those who are inside can enjoy the attractions of the park without rubbing elbows. It is to be appreciated that the authorities refuse to make extra money and offer those inside an experience free from congested parking lots, trails, ferries, and restaurants.

We hardly accept the reality that, although we are so close to Many Glacier, we can't visit it. At least now, we know what to do on a later return. We drown our disappointment in large portions of huckleberry pie at Two Sisters Café and then head back to the side of the park we have just left. To sweeten us even more, fate puts in our way a bear cub that eats blueberries very close to the side of the road. We stop to watch and video discreetly without disturbing the cub in any way... along with about ten other cars behind us.

It is just past noon, and we have plenty of time before heading to Helena, Montana. We park at the first panoramic point we encounter, and then go down the trail that leads to one of the dozens of lakes in the area. We arrive at a lodgepole pine forest that is somehow dead and alive at the same time, which makes us stop and look at it closely. As far as the eye can see, charred trunks stand straight and black above the green hills. Flowers in vivid colors grow among them in contrast to a world that had ceased to exist once the fires had consumed their flames. These trees, with burned bodies and still strong roots are called *the standing dead.* It makes sense why. They aren't cut down but in fact remain an important part of the forest, and they retain their role in the ecosystem for fauna and flora.

The next generation of forests replaces the burned one we have passed so far. However, there is no sign of sprouting here, which convinces us that the wildfire was recent and only grass and wildflowers have grown from its ashes. Certainly, in a few years young pines will show their tender tops at the feet of their ancestors. For now, you must have an extremely optimistic disposition to see beyond this forest cemetery.

Just a week after our departure, massive fires engulfed tens of square miles of forest due to lightning, forcing the authorities to close the part of the park we had just visited.

At mile 10,195, we checked in at the Quality Inn, Helena, room 320, with small regrets for everything we failed to see. But we are grateful for the serene day we spent in a fantastic corner of the world and for how much we managed to learn about it. Our enthusiasm level is much lower now, and this is only because there are four nights and four days left until the end of our *American Vacation.* There is still so much more to see in this fabulous country. I know. We should be happy with everything we managed to see, and we are. But the nostalgia we feel towards the end is real and hard to ignore.

# CHAPTER XI
## - *WYOMING, FOREVER WEST*

# 39 - *YELLOWSTONE NATIONAL PARK, MADISON CAMPGROUND, WY*

W e dedicated two days to the world's oldest national park, Yellowstone. Just looking at its resume we realize that maybe twenty days would be the correct amount of time to spend here. In all the national or state parks we have visited this month and a half, we could have stayed at least five times longer than we did. However, in the limited time we had, M. wanted to show me as many of his favorite places on the North American continent and visit a few together for the first time. He couldn't have planned the whole thing better. Maybe in a future that will be generous to us, we will return to the places that attracted us the most and will be able to say that we have walked all their paths. Until then though, if this then will exist, the travel diary I wrote along and across the North American map is a valuable memory and an authentic read.

Yellowstone is the birthplace of the idea of a national park. This happened no later than 1872 when the urgent need to protect the 3,471 square miles of the land of fire, ice, and wild animals had arisen. Since then, Americans have begun to identify, preserve, and manage naturally rich spaces for the benefit of the land, the wildlife, the public and the pure joy of future generations.

In their eager desire for exploitation and expansion, however, they had eyes to see that some lands were far too valuable to be parceled out and sold. It was concluded that these domains were, in fact, a legacy to all humankind, places reserved for knowledge and the possibility of reconnecting with the origin of all things.

I am thinking of my country and the hundreds of places that could benefit from this philosophy but which have no chance to be protected for reasons closely linked to ignorance, indifference, and corruption. However, it is fantastic to discover that in this wide world, the same does not happen everywhere, and it makes it even more unreal for me to have been a witness to such behavior.

It's obvious that it wasn't the American government that first discovered the richness of this territory but the native tribes who had lived here 11,000 years ago. There are over 1,000 archeological sites in this park attesting to the existence of the ancestors of the Blackfeet, Flathead, Cayuse, Coeur d'Alene, Bannock, Nez Perce, Shoshone, and Umatilla tribes. Over the centuries, there had been around twenty-six tribes who were calling Yellowstone their home. The two that still live here, Blackfeet and Flathead, keep in touch with the federal government through their representatives and contribute to every decision involving the development of the park.

Within the 3,471 square mile perimeter, for millions of years, there have been mountain ranges, valleys, forests, lakes, canyons, and rivers, all above the largest active volcano on the continent, which is also the star of this park. The Caldera Volcano has erupted several times in the last two million years, petrifying forests and covering considerable areas with layers of solid volcanic rocks through which gush many geysers and hot springs.

Thanks to these exceptional geographical and geological details, the park has always attracted visitors reaching one million in 1948 and over four million in 2016. Nothing about Yellowstone is common, and this becomes very clear to us as soon as we approach it.

At the northwestern entrance from Bozeman, Montana, there are four queues with hundreds of cars waiting in line. A man in a uniform, emblem, and wide brim hat passes by each car and asks the driver if they have a pass. If so, the driver is to prepare it together with an identification. If not, they must have exact cash or a credit card handy so things will run smoothly and quickly to avoid downtime. This is an example of impeccable attitude and organization offered to tourists that I have ever experienced, and I am again amazed that such a thing exists somewhere in the world.

We first stop at the Roosevelt Arch, the monument-symbol of the park, a massive stone and brick arch fifty feet high on top of which the message, *"for the benefit and enjoyment of the people"* stands for everyone to see.

Just a few miles further from the entrance, we reach Wyoming, Forever West. 95% of the park spreads on its territory. For the first part of the day, we choose about seven miles of trails that take us through a surreal setting, in which colors in intense tones remind me of the spice markets in Asia and of the Van Gogh's Blue Period. We visit them one by one: Mammoth Hot Springs Area Trail, Norris Geyser Basin Complete Loop Trail, and Mud Volcano Trail. These three areas abound in hot springs, geysers, and muddy volcanoes, all with wide wooden boardwalks raised above the ground.

Everywhere we look, green and turquoise water stains the white of the limestone, and streaks of cinnamon, paprika, turmeric, and mustard create abstract art on a canvas of honey and milk. We walk among the clouds of steam sneezing from underground galleries, oversized ashtrays where charred trees shake their ashes, and deep puddles of clay and mud that bubble at boiling temperatures. A heterogeneous river of tourists flows over the porous rock terraces that sweat boiling water soaked in sulfur. Nothing seems familiar from the footbridge. Not the shape, the color, the sound, nor the smell. Only the forests and mountains in the distance look perfectly like rocks and trees and easily resonate in my memory. The rest is novelty and extravagance that I can only describe with the senses.

In the afternoon, we descended a steep trail to the Lower Falls of the Yellowstone River, the waterfall with the largest volume of water in the Rocky Mountains. We arrive right above the spot where the river overflows down the mountain face, after dozens of switchbacks that flatten my toes in the tip of the boots. Halfway through, we intersect with a group of paramedics carrying a man on a stretcher. We are not able to find out what happened, but again I am deeply impressed by the impeccable services in these parks.

At the end of the path, a huge concrete balcony with metal railings holds dozens of tourists who stand together and watch the Yellowstone River flowing noisily and wet from a height of over 300 feet into the Grand Canyon of the Yellowstone. To have the opportunity of witnessing the exact moment, when a waterfall creates itself perpetually, is another thing that I have to add to the long list of firsts on this trip.

Looking against the torrent, a few miles above, you can see the same river pouring another waterfall down the valley. That is the Upper Falls of the Yellowstone. It starts at the lake of the same name and waters the entire Hayden Valley. The view is monumental, as is the way back that takes us up to the parking lot on the same dozens of sloping curves that force the air out of my lungs and make me blow like a bicycle pump. Luckily, a woman who screams at me admiringly, *"Your hair is stinking cute!"* gives me a bit more energy for the climb and for a very faint, *"Thank you!"* and a smile.

On the way to Madison Campground where the tent spot number F22 is waiting for us, we pass through Hayden Valley, where I see for the first time a herd of wild bison. Traffic slows down considerably because everyone wants to see the animals up close. I am also curious. I stick my head up to my waist through the sunroof to see them better and to be able to take some pictures.

The bison are extremely exotic: massive, hooded, bearded, busty, with strong front legs and ridiculously thin hind legs. We wonder why they don't fall on their heads with such unequal distributed proportions. Even more interesting is that they can swim at their large size and proof of that is one bison crossing the Yellowstone River without sinking right before our eyes. We applaud and marvel at the athletic performance of the largest mammals on the North American continent. In the morning, when we roll out of the tent, we imitate their roars and have a lot of fun conjugating the verb *to roar*.

At mile 10,503, we enter the campground and start setting up the tent before nightfall. We then prepare a royal salad with

Thousand Island dressing for both lunch and dinner and eat it by the lamplight, watching the campfires that illuminate the forest from all directions. Opposite us, a large group of adults and children sit comfortably in folding chairs, forming a wide circle around the fire pit and embodying the ideal vacation picture.

The commotion and merriment that pervades their group, and the warm light of the fire, convinces us to light up the wood left by the former tenants in the fire pit. This completes the ambiance of a perfect evening under the Yellowstone sky. Before sleep claims me, I finish Waking up in a Tent and fall asleep thinking of old age, which doesn't seem to scare anyone more than it scares me.

# 40 - *YELLOWSTONE NATIONAL PARK, MADISON CAMPGROUND, WY*

I become aware that I have a good day ahead of me right from the early morning in the park public restroom where I witness a memorable life sequence. A few-year-old girl comes out of the toilet, washes her hands, and then starts brushing her teeth, letting the water run. Her mother turns off the tap, lifts the little girl and places her on the countertop by the sink, then tells her:

*"Honey, water is very precious and we must not waste it. Water is important for our planet and we should be careful with it. Whenever you are in the bathroom brushing your teeth or showering, only let the water run for as long as you use it and turn it off when you don't. This way you save water."*

That a lesson in ecology and parenting takes place in a seemingly insignificant scene in a public restroom in a Wyoming campground, tells me so much about this society. I am no longer surprised I have never seen traces of garbage thrown on the ground in these public areas. All the parks are equipped with enough bins, and almost everywhere, one can recycle. I have not seen people step off of the trail, defecate in the woods, or light fires wherever they want. People are polite, helpful, and always careful not to bother anybody. Whenever we intersect with families with children, invariably one of the parents tells the kids to step to the right to give us room to pass. It is such a relief to know that such a society exists, that it is not a utopia.

The day also promises temperatures that are still low and pleasant. The Park is almost a hundred miles wide from one side to the other. It takes us about an hour to descend south to the Upper Geyser Basin where there are no less than 160 geysers, out of 500 in Yellowstone, including the Old Faithful, the most famous geyser in the world.

First, we enter the Old Faithful Visitor Center (one of the ten information centers in the park) to find out when the next eruption will take place. An electronic panel tells us that it happens once approximately every ninety minutes. We have close to a half-hour until the next show. So, we get closer to Old Faithful to find a good place from where we can see and film it without any impediments. It turns out we do the right thing. In front of the geyser, at about 300 feet, the long area bordered with benches set out for visitors is already three-quarters occupied. We sit across from it right in the middle of the row on the curb of the footbridge, in front of the benches. Then we wait as the stands crowd more and more until it probably exceeds 1,000 people.

At the promised hour (+/- three minutes), a splendor of a fountain shoots from the ground splashing water about 150 feet up in the air for a few good minutes to the applause and cheers of the audience.

It is impressive what nature knows what to do when it's constrained. Old Faithful is a cone-shaped geyser, something common in the world of geologists. What makes it special though, is that somewhere in its conical throat a large piece of rock got stuck during an earthquake hundreds of millions of years ago. Therefore, the water keeps gathering under the pressure of the obstacle, and once every ninety minutes it is released in a spectacular way, which deserves public applause. It is the first geyser discovered by the first explorers of the area, around 1870 and the first to receive a name.

We then enter the Upper Geyser Basin and the Old Faithful Geyser Observation Loop Trail, a route of more than four miles that offers tourists access to the area with the highest concentration of geysers in the world. Old Faithful is the icing on the volcanic cake. However, in this basin, four more of them erupt at measured intervals and compete in age, size, height, or duration of eruption. The four geysers are Castle, Daisy, Grand, and Riverside, but the list continues with hot springs, natural pools, and other geysers brought to the surface by twisted volcanic arteries that stretch tens of miles in all directions. The most important ones can be easily identified, and the names are surprisingly close to their aesthetic reality: Crested Pool, Firehole River, Economic Geyser, Chromatic and Beauty Pool, Grotto Geyser, Comet and Splendid Geysers, The Punch Bowl-Black Sand Basin, Morning Glory Pool, Spasmodic Pool, Beehive, and Anemone Pool.

We find the same creamy intense colors from yesterday in the pictures we take today, and they never cease to amaze us with the contrast between this above-ground-aquatic world around which plants and trees grow as if nothing unusual was happening in the neighborhood.

Another unusual thing catches my eye during our morning walk. It is in the form of a disposable-lidded cup that seems to be full of hot coffee, which I see at intermittent intervals in the hands of fellow visitors. It is clear that coffee is sold somewhere nearby. So, I hurry up and pull M. by the hand to the Visitor Center where I see a long line in front of a cafe. No matter how long it takes, I cannot leave here without a cup of hot coffee. Ambitious as I am, I achieve this in just twenty minutes. Then, sitting comfortably in an armchair with wide armrests placed in front of the window facing the Old Faithful, we admire a new artistic act of the old geyser. With the coffee burning my fingertips, it is much more spectacular.

We move on, but not before bringing *Waking up in a Tent* out of the car and leaving it on one of the window seats. Surely, someone will be happy to find it and maybe read it. I thought that would be a better fate than taking it home and keeping it on a shelf for the next ten years. I promised *Wild* to one of my friends, so I will take that one back with me.

Our next stop is the Midway Geyser Basin Trail, where the queen of the ball is the Grand Prismatic Hot Spring, the largest hot spring in the United States. Astonishment, wonder, surprise, admiration, and all the synonyms of being amazed reach levels of shock when the wooden path brings us to the edge of this body of water where the artist used all the colors of the rainbow for a psychedelic make-up. The navy-blue middle is like a mesmerizing iris that gradually fades into turquoise, blue, and green. The edge contrasts sharply with the water, coloring the shore in layers of yellow, orange, brick red, and dark brown.

The lake formed by the hot spring is about 160 feet deep, has a diameter of 370 feet and the water comes to the surface almost at a boiling temperature, but it cools towards the shore. It seems that this is one of the explanations of the color spectrum. In the middle of it, the water retains its natural clear color because of the total lack of living organisms. As it cools outwards, all sorts of bacteria and microorganisms that pigment it so intensely populate it. This is the scientific information gathered from the information panels on the spot, but any explanation seems somehow outdated by the fact that it is the most unreal place I have ever had the chance to see. And I have seen quite a few lately.

I reinforce the idea that the human mind is far too limited to comprehend the wonders of this world. All along this vacation, I lived with the feeling that I would need a much larger memory to be able to keep safe what I saw and experienced. Now, I have this book that will save my trip from the viruses of oblivion and that will also arouse curiosity in all those who will venture out west.

On the way to West Thumb Geyser Basin, we hit the brakes and back up in front of Lake Isa, which catches our eye with the hundreds of yellow water lilies that float elegantly on a lake at 8,262 feet of altitude. They are more specifically Yellow Pond Lily, a variety of water lilies that live in the lower part of the Rocky Mountains. Honestly, we did not expect to find water lilies in Yellowstone, but nothing can surprise us here. They are as unique as the geysers and hot springs that gush straight from the Yellowstone Lake and its shore, along the West Thumb Basin route.

We walk on the bank, through a large hydrothermal area where hot springs form wide deep lakes, with the clear water of a turquoise stolen from another world, through which you can see to their base. At a trail intersection, where the boardwalk widens in front of a deep pool the color of mouthwash, a group of tourists listens to a ranger who says:

*"Repeat after me: Blue is not for you!"*

*"Blue is not for you,"* about thirty people repeated a few times, so that's clear to them that no matter how attractive the water of the thermal lakes may appear, it is not what it seems. It is downright lethal. Many accidents that ended in severe burns have happened here over the years, because despite the signs that warn visitors of the dangers and advise them to stay on the trails, there are curious people who step down from the boardwalks and want to touch the water. That is probably why the rangers want to reinforce the written messages with a few impactful words, slipped into speeches about the formation of these sources. Even the names of the thermal pools are more than self-explanatory: Abyss, Black, Collapsing, and Perforated Pool.

Just as Yosemite, Yellowstone is full of traveling families, mostly Americans, Indians, and Asians. I saw many South Americans in Yosemite and almost none here. From time to time, we hear people speaking French, but we don't know if they are from Canada or France. American tourist families appear to have at least three children, often even four and between two and four grandparents. If the parents are young, it is possible for the mother to be pregnant and for the father to carry a one-year-old child in a baby carrier while holding hands with a four-year-old.

From young to old, everyone is properly dressed and shod. I have much respect for all the parents who teach their young children to go out in nature and find out as much as possible about it. In my country, I rarely see such a thing, so much so that I believe it does not exist.

What I haven't seen much of this vacation are smokers. I don't think I need two hands to count the ones I did see. One would suffice. I smoked for more than ten years of my life. So, it is not about good or bad, but about the fact that this habit is not widespread in tourist areas. Here, in the US, you can't even smoke outside or wherever you feel like it, but only in specially arranged areas. In my country, you can smoke on the patios of restaurants and mainly anywhere as long as it is outside. However, that is not the case here.

Before lunch, we make a short stop on a sandy tongue of land that divides the waters of Yellowstone Lake into a picturesque bay, where I take off my shoes to feel the sand between my toes.

Then we visited Tower Falls by descending a short steep trail. Tower Creek, before flowing into the Yellowstone River, shows independence and originality. It throws itself into a waterfall of about 125 feet, among thousands of rock pinnacles, very similar to the hoodoos from Bryce Canyon, but thinner and with rounded tops. Again, we are not surprised to find such a thing in Yellowstone, where all the wonders of nature seem to have gathered.

Also, on the high steep bank on which Tower Creek flows, after rolling spectacularly down the valley, I notice some rock formations resembling the hexagonal rocks of the Giant's Causeway in Northern Ireland. They appear to have been planted by the hands of a superhero - that's how aligned and straight they are, as a natural fence.

On the trail, descending to the vista point from where we watch the waterfall, we meet a German-speaking mother with two children holding her hand and a seven-year-old girl on her arms, sucking her finger and trying to fall asleep. Such an outing seems exhausting for both mother and children, but not impossible, as I clearly witness.

We postpone lunch a bit, as we always do, crossing the Lamar Valley, well known for its abundance of wildlife. We stop on the side of the road in a parking lot where we wait a while until a spot clears out. Then, we go on the edge of the Lamar River to wade a little in the water. Next to it, bison and wild geese wet their fur and feathers without disturbing each other, and in the distance, a pack of wolves probably plot a night attack.

Time passes, as does lunchtime, so we make a stop at Roosevelt Lodge and Cabins for *linner*. Everything is so lovely here that I never want to leave this place. The cottage-style restaurant, built out of massive logs and wooden floors in 1903 in honor of President Theodore Roosevelt's visit to the region, offers impeccable service, good food, and a gift shop with artisanal objects and tribal jewelry. It also has a large veranda on which about fifteen rocking chairs are swinging tirelessly under napping, reading, or just chilling-out customers. We too tried them after dinner, me with a Mammoth Lemonade cocktail in hand, and M. empty-handed as he is the designated driver. We watch the mountains in the distance with a smile of total relaxation on our faces.

There is nothing to say here, just to breathe the strong mountain air and engrave deep in our memory the charm of this place. In front of the porch, a chipmunk frantically rummages for its dinner and finds it in the form of a dried leaf fallen into the grass. It picks it up, and it is bigger than its head. It runs to the corner of the lodge, constantly looking left and right so that no one can grab it, Then, turning its back, it nibbles loudly on it.

On the way to Bridge Bay Campground, we pass through Hayden Valley once more, where we expect to find traffic due to maybe a bison that fell asleep in the middle of the road or a herd of elk lost on the asphalt. This time, however, hundreds of cars are standing still because a bear with two cubs is walking on the side of the road. Of course, everyone wants to see and photograph them. People get out of their cars with the cameras ready and approach them as much as their courage allows, but much less than they are advised at the entrance to the park, meaning a hundred yards. I do the same, step out of the car, and head to the valley where the other people are already coming back. I see the cutest grizzly bear cub trying to catch up with its mother and brother or sister who had descended deeper into the forest.

We continue on the edge of some pine forests burned maybe ten years ago, which already have new generations of young ones grown among the sharp and black trunks. Just like everywhere else, we see forests affected by fires. Burned, torn down, or overturned trees lay exactly where they ended up so that they can continue to contribute to the well-being of the ecosystem. Maybe that is why the forests here look much wilder than back home, where they immediately remove the fallen wood.

At mile 10,663, we park inside Bridge Bay Campground on tent site number F280. The campground is located north of Yellowstone Lake, near Bridge Bay Marina. From where we are, we can see the road that borders the lake and the wooded peaks of the Absaroka Mountain Range. A magical place for one last night in a tent. Two elks eat grass on the side of the road, and squirrels and chipmunks look like Christmas decorations in the pine tree behind the tent.

A park employee walks among the tents and the RVs announcing tonight's ranger speech that will take place at 9:30 pm in the campground amphitheater. The theme is, "Ranger Talks – The Milky Way." I would like to go as I am also very curious how these events take place, but we are tired and have an extremely early morning ahead of us. We prefer to snuggle into our two-sleeping-bags-turned-into-one (ever since the first night in the tent) and take a retrospective of our vacation.

*"I can't believe I climbed White Mountain!"* I say proudly.

*"Yes, you did, but it's no big deal. You'll climb others like Mount Whitney, which is only twice as hard to climb,"* replies M. confidently, believing in me once again, But this time it feels like Whitney is really out of my league, no matter how much M. believes in me.

*"Hm, I don't know what to say... I told you, White was my Everest, and that's enough for me. I am up for normal, moderate trails, hard enough but still fun. Walking twenty miles without being able to breathe normally is not fun,"* I try to convince M. that everything beyond White I'll leave for professionals.

*"You'll get used to it. You'll climb Mount White a few more times for training, and you won't have that breathing problem anymore,"* M. insists.

*"I don't think so, we'll see... But anyway, one thing is clear - I like camping,"* I take the discussion in another direction.

*"Yes, but it's so much more fun sleeping in a tent in the snow,"* M. joggles with the conversation and brings it back.

*"And I like going on mountain trails, not necessarily so demanding,"* I insist ignoring the detour.

"*Yes, but it's nicer in the winter, on the glacier,*" he raises the bets.

"*It would be nice to walk in the forest in the morning, about three miles, like a daily exercise,*" I tone it down.

"*Yes, but it's much nicer to run about seven miles uphill every day...*"

Generally, this is how our discussions about the embrace of nature go. At least until today they ended with my attempts to overcome my comfort zone and go figure, all the attempts were successful. On these occasions, I have tested my limits. It is very clear to me now what I am willing and eager to do to discover the world around me.

What is even clearer to me is that I will not read *The Cook*, Henry Miller's first novel, just because I bought it from a place so special to me. Some things remain symbolic because they are far below our expectations. I will always remember this book, in which Miller tested his literary-linguistic skills, and I twisted my imagination to exhaustion trying to follow his writing. I reserve my admiration for the Black Spring[23] and *Henry and June*[24].

# CHAPTER XII - *SOUTH DAKOTA, GREAT FACES, GREAT PLACES*

# 41 - *MOUNT RUSHMORE NATIONAL MEMORIAL, WALL, SD*

W e leave Yellowstone and aim east. There are sections of the road under construction, so all the cars going in the opposite directions have to take turns sharing a single lane. A man directs the traffic and waves goodbye to us as we leave the park. I wave back.

We exit the Shoshone National Forest and enter the Buffalo Bill Reservoir Dam area, where the Shoshone River is trapped in a lake to be used for electricity, irrigation, and flood prevention. The landscape is lively on the shore, with tents and RVs, picnic areas with rooftops, and access to water. It may be the last stop before Yellowstone for tourists driving west.

All over America, I have seen RVs of all shapes and sizes. The most attractive are the ones rented from *Cruise America*, because they are wallpapered with images from national parks, relatively small, white, and in one piece. Then, there are others just like these, but big as buses and very difficult to pass. The most common of them are those in the form of a small, large, or very large caravan, towed by pickup trucks. All have yacht names: *Catalina, Jamboree, Four Winds, Sun Searcher, White Water, El Monte, Big Country, Bounder, Wildwood, Forest River, Cyclone, Allegro*, etc. Most RVs are expandable and when parked in campsites, increase their capacity by another 30% either sideways or above. We camped next to such a caravan in Redwoods National Park Campground and as much as we could manage to see from the outside, on the inside it looked like a luxury yacht.

We continue our journey east for another 150 miles. There is nothing to see but the road and the sky. At one point, we cross the town of Ten Sleep, which consists of the main street, a bar, a restaurant, a museum, and an RV campground. A woman is sitting on a picnic bench and playing the guitar. A mother and a little girl are walking down the deserted street holding ice cream cones. We pass this human settlement wondering if it was just an illusion, so quickly appearing and disappearing beyond our car windows.

Then, we are alone again on US-16. I notice Wyoming means vast desert areas, covered with badlands and dotted with rock formations of red stone just like in Arizona. The further east we go, the road climbs to 10,000 feet in altitude. There are pine forests, hills, and fast streams, lakes, and ski resorts.

Winters are heavy here, so at about a hundred yards parallel to the highway some panels prevent snow from reaching the road in large amounts. We then descend and arrive in Buffalo, a small town with pretty houses, lawnmowers, porch swings, flowerpots by the front door, and no fences. Then again, deserted hills run for as far as we can see.

We enter the I90 and head in the direction of Mount Rushmore. We pass Gillette, Wyoming, where they drill for oil, and then Newcastle where deer graze on the side of the road. A few deer have crossed the road right in front of us and look disoriented and also out of place in this woodless background. Since this morning, we have covered 330 miles of completely random charm.

We enter South Dakota at mile 11,079 and at the same time, the Black Hills National Forest. We turn right, get out of the car, and M. sits victoriously under the state sign. At the entrance and exit of each state, on the right side of the road, there are panels saying, *"Welcome to..."* or *"See you soon,"* usually showing the state flag or slogan. In this case, the sign displays four American presidents sculpted in the mountain. South Dakota, Great Faces, Great Places, is the only state M. has not yet visited. He now closes the circle with a solemn moment witnessed by another man who's just as excited as M.

*"South Dakota was my unicorn,"* says M., smiling at the man next to him.

*"Oh, congratulations!"* he replies, used to chatty fellow travelers.

*"It was the last state, and now I've seen all the contiguous states!"* M. continues proudly, justifying his enthusiasm.

*"Impressive! Great job!"* offers the man with thumbs up.

We move on, after taking some photos in which M., The Conqueror, leisurely consumes the glorious moment.

The area with forested hills gradually increases in touristic degrees. Immediately after Custer, we start seeing cabins, restaurants, hotels, and gift shops along the road. Billboards urge us to turn right towards Crazy Horse, but not knowing about the existence of this place, we miss the second impressive monument in the area, Crazy Horse Memorial. I see in passing a human profile carved in white stone somewhere up in the distance, but I tell myself that I must be mistaken. I am not... Many weeks later, looking at the pictures and checking the map, I realized that just thirty miles before Mount Rushmore, the famous Crazy Horse stands carved in the stone of Thunderhead Mountain. It is considered holy land, because the warrior Oglala Lakota (the one whom the monument honors) is an important historical figure in the Native American culture. The massive sculpture has been in operation since 1948, and the sketch depicts the tribal chief riding a horse with his left arm outstretched, pointing into the distance. At the moment, only the face is finished, but if it were completed in its entirety, it would become the second tallest sculpture in the world, after the Statue of Liberty. We deeply regret failing to visit the site, but we add it to the list and hope to see it next time.

As a child, I had often caught glimpses of Mount Rushmore in movies and every time I thought the image must be made on the computer, that such a sculpture cannot be real, that man is not able to make a masterpiece of such proportions. I grew up and discovered that it does exist, but now that the profiles of the four presidents are a few hundred yards away, it seems just as unreal to me.

I read on the information panels that the monument stretches over a two square mile area and that 400 workers had labored at an altitude of 5,700 feet, for over fourteen years to make it happen. The initial goal of this work was to increase tourism in the Black Hills Mountain area, an objective that had long exceeded its ambition, currently bringing over two million tourists here annually. However, over time, it has become more of a historical monument than a touristic one, and you can feel it from the entrance.

The access to the stands, from where you can see the massive sculpture, is through the Avenue of Flags. The path is bordered by pillars bearing the flags of the fifty states and the name and date when each became American territory. I have a rather disturbing feeling, kind of patriotic envy, a desire to be part of an equally proud nation, which can attract people from all over the world through its achievements.

The ambitious project created by Gutzon Borglum (a former student of Auguste Rodin[25]) and completed by his son, brings out the iconic figures of George Washington, Thomas Jefferson, Abraham Lincoln, and Theodore Roosevelt. These four presidents symbolize the birth, growth, development, and protection of the United States. The plan, which began in 1927, involved making the four models from the waist up. After America joined World War II, in 1941, the work stopped at the stage it is now and has since been declared completed.

As we leave the park, we go to the Visitor Center to buy some souvenirs and mark my travel diary with the Rushmore Monument stamp. Almost all national and state parks have a stamp in the visitor centers with the date and name of the park, which is usually used on scouts notebooks and postcards.

Walking through the museum-shop-visitor center, we witness an adorable moment. A little boy of six or seven years of age, hands the employee a scout's notebook and tells her that he has completed everything and that he is ready for the oath. They both raise their right hand, and the little boy repeats the following promise after the woman:

*"As a Junior Ranger, I promise to teach others about what I have learned today, explore other parks and historic sites, and help preserve and protect these places, so future generations can enjoy them."*

Applause, hugs, blushing, excited parents. Enthusiastic about the small event, we study a little about what happens in this program for Junior Rangers. We find out that the entire park system in the United States provides children between the ages of five and twelve a well thought out program of outdoor activities that familiarize them with the specifics of places. At the end of all activities, they receive a badge or emblem to wear proudly on the scout's vest. This way, children spend time in nature, socialize, learn various details about the environment and are rewarded only if they have the lists checked in full. Brilliant.

At mile 11,202, we carry our luggage into room number 11 at the Super 8 Motel in Wall, South Dakota. This occasion marks the last night of our trip. I feel that I will need time to put my thoughts in order and arrange every memory in its own drawer.

Tomorrow is the forty-fifth day since I embarked on the adventure of my life with my dear M., and I will return rich and fully happy. I wish this North American vacation won't end, so this is why I will share everything I was lucky enough to see and experience in a travel book for people around the world who wish to visit this incredible land. I am kind of a Junior Ranger myself!

# CHAPTER XIII -
## *MINNESOTA, THE STATE OF TEN THOUSAND LAKES ☼ WISCONSIN, AMERICA'S DAIRYLAND*

# 42 - *BADLANDS NATIONAL PARK, SD* ☼ *GILBERTS, IL*

I t is the morning of the last day of the trip, and the day is crying with us, raining small and warm tears. We are in Badlands National Park, South Dakota, walking the trails of a landscape horizontally striped in light gray and pink, applied evenly over endless hills of sedimentary rocks eroded in sharp peaks and wide canyons. At first glance, we seem to be in the middle of an arid rocky area. But every few hundred yards we find patches of ground covered with healthy grass, where herds of bighorn sheep graze carelessly, and bluebirds fly, unreal, among high bundles of wild sunflowers.

We moved through the same rain that wished us good luck a month and a half ago in Illinois and now seems to be saying goodbye. It rains without stopping for twelve hours straight, as long as it takes us to cross three-quarters of South Dakota, all of Minnesota, and a corner of Wisconsin, where a double rainbow sits as a finish line at the end of the highway. As the sky weeps so diligently for the end of our vacation, we skip whining about it and take back to Illinois everything we remember from the last forty-five days and nights spent in the American West.

Coming from a country of a few highways, maybe less than a hundred miles in total, I find the North American infrastructure a road paradise. No matter what state we have been in for the last forty-five days, roads, highways, interstates, and routes have taken us over the most diverse landforms, in impeccable conditions. There are exceptions, of course, but only due to isolation or high altitude - well paved, well maintained, signposted, marked, and solid under our wheels in good or weeping weather like today. This is the norm around here, and it is all for the benefit of the people.

At mile 11,815, we stop in La Crosse, Wisconsin, for a *lupper* at Arby's. We eat curly fries and brisket sandwiches as we drive eighty miles per hour on the wet night-covered highway. When we park in front of our friends' house in Gilberts, Illinois, the car display shows 12,255 miles or 19,790 kilometers.

# 43 - *CHICAGO O'HARE INTERNATIONAL AIRPORT, USA → AVRAM IANCU INTERNATIONAL AIRPORT CLUJ, ROMANIA, EUROPE*

M . says that a good story always ends in the airport bar, and if I remember correctly the few flights home from Chicago, he is right. People who come and go from one of the largest airports in the States bring with them stories from all over the world, just as we head home with one full of events from the American West. This time we have almost two hours before takeoff. So, we make ourselves comfortable at the bar (don't sit at a table or you'll lose all the fun) and order a Samuel Adams beer for M. and a margarita for me.

Once every half hour, the bar colleagues give the baton to new, thirsty ones. Today, we have next to us on our right a woman in her seventies with whom M. has been talking ever since he sat down and ordered the first glass of beer. A simple *"cheers"* is enough to open a conversation at the airport, and then everything follows naturally:

*"Cheers! Have a good flight!"* M. takes the floor.

*"Oh, thank you! You too. Where are you flying today?"* answers the woman.

*"We're going to Romania,"* I jumped in, always excited to talk to new people.

*"Well, that's too much of a coincidence! I'm flying to Israel now, but Romania is next on my list of travels,"* the woman exclaims enthusiastically.

*"Wow, that's just incredible that you're going to Israel... I'd like to go there myself one day,"* a man from the right joins in.

*"Yes, it's true, my husband just goes on and on about Israel,"* the gentleman's wife interrupts him.

*"And where are you off to today?"* M. asks the spouses.

*"We're traveling to Dublin, Ireland for a wedding. My wife's best friend is getting married to an Irish man,"* says the husband.

*"You won't believe it, but I'm flying to Beirut for my sister's engagement party,"* replies unexpectedly a guy who takes the old

lady's place after we all wish her safe travels.

*"I just found out about it last week, and the only ticket I could buy on such short notice gets me through Dubai, and it will take an entire day to arrive at my sister's,"* goes the new guy.

*"Wow, that's a long trip… Hang in there. Have another beer then,"* proposes the Irish bride's friend. *"And how about you guys, where have you been?"* She addresses us.

*"We've spent a month and a half in the West, doing all the national parks over there and then the Pacific Coast up to Cape Flattery and then back here,"* M. summarizes.

*"That's amazing, you guys! That's something we should do, honey, when we'll have enough time for this kind of travel,"* she replies, imagining how awesome that would be.

Even at the airport, globetrotters confirm that I have lived something many people with a traveling soul wish for, so I return home relieved and happy. I think I was 50% lucky to go on such an adventure and 50% willing to do it. I saw incredible places and lived unique experiences, but none of this would have happened if my desire for novelty had not mixed with a real availability. Most places and experiences required more of me physically and mentally to an extent that I had to overcome barriers of resistance and tolerance. I was always aware of my limits, but I overcame them all with amazement, sincerely shocked to discover that I can do much more than I am aware. I will increase the percentage of luck to 75%, because I had M. by my side with his young and fearless spirit and his courage infected me. I had brought with me a substantial dose of unconsciousness and playfulness, and together with the borrowed courage and desire for knowledge, I solved equations with unknown exponents from *19* states, *33* national and state parks, *170* miles of hiking, and *7* landforms, along a *12,255* mile stretch of road.

[1] John Steinbeck Travels with Charley in Search of America; Penguin Classics Deluxe Edition; 1986. Part ONE, pg. 8

[2] Shrimp (Spanish)

[3] The United Nations Educational, Scientific and Cultural Organization

[4] Beautiful, isn't it? (Romanian)

[5] Rafael Nadal Parera is a Spanish professional tennis player

[6] Mountain resorts in Transylvania, Romania

[7] John Robert Fowles (31 March, 1926 – 5 November, 2005) was an international renown English novelist

[8] City in Romania

[9] A group selfie, where someone takes a picture of themselves with other people in the shot

[10] A column or pinnacle of weathered rock

[11] Natural rock formations in the Bucegi Natural Park, Romania

[12] Sacred geometry ascribes symbolic and sacred meanings to certain geometric shapes and proportions. It is associated with the belief that a god is the geometer of the world.

[13] Bill Bryson – "The Lost Continent – Travels in small-town America", eBook, 1989

[14] Waking Up in a Tent: Empty Nest on the Pacific Crest Trail, 2017, by Laurel Siegel Gord

[15] Pacific Crest Trail

[16] Henry Valentine Miller (December 26, 1891 – June 7, 1980) was an American writer and artist

[17] Mircea Eliade (March 13, 1907 – April 22, 1986) was a Romanian historian of religion, fiction writer, philosopher, and professor at the University of Chicago

[18] Oscar Fingal O'Flahertie Wills Wilde was an Irish poet and playwright

[19] Angela Anaïs Juana Antolina Rosa Edelmira Nin y Culmell (February 21, 1903 – January 14, 1977), known professionally as Anaïs Nin, was a French-Cuban-American diarist, essayist, novelist and writer of short stories and erotica

[20] "Trash the dress" photos are pictures taken after the wedding in which the bride essentially ruins her dress.

[21] A 1990 American fantasy romance film

[22] A meal between lunch and dinner, also known as lupper

[23] Black Spring, novel by Henry Miller

[24] Henry and June, novel by Henry Miller

[25] François Auguste René Rodin (12 November 1840 – 17 November 1917) was a French sculptor generally considered the founder of modern sculpture.

# ABOUT THE AUTHOR

## Raluca Barbu

Raluca Barbu (former Marchiş) is a published author in Romania who relocated to the United States of America in 2019. She now lives with her daughter and husband in Illinois. Apart from writing, she has worked for more than fifteen years in sales, public relations, and marketing for some of the most influential companies in Romania.

She has also written for LaPunkt.ro as a movie critic, for Apostrof, the Romanian Writers' Union magazine, and Acribia, the Librarianship College paper in Cluj-Napoca, Romania (back in the 2000s). For five consecutive years she wrote social and cultural pieces on her own platform, ralucabarbu.ro, which later became her fourth book, Terapie prin scris (Writing Therapy).

Her latest book, American Vacation. 12,000 Miles Into the Wild West is a travel book about the United States and its most iconic Western landmarks, seen through the eyes of a Romanian writer. It is in many respects one-of-a-kind because no other Romanian author has traveled and wrote about the American West. It provides a foreign writer's take on the American landscape and tourism through the eyes of a former citizen of a communist country. It is a homage given both to the beauty of the American outdoors and to the way nature is respected and preserved by the authorities and visitors. What makes it special though is the travel narrative that Raluca has brought back as a literary genre. In a world of Google reviews, travel blogs, and vacation guides she manages to shine a light on the lost art of travel memoirs.

# BOOKS BY THIS AUTHOR

## Oraşul Din Viaţa Mea (My City Within)

Memoir on surviving life as a YA. Grinta Publishing House, Cluj-Napoca, Romania, 2007

## Corporatistul (The Corporate Man)

Novel about losing and finding oneself while working for a multinational corporation. Tracus Arte Publishing House, Bucharest, Romania, 2012

## Selfie În Oglindă. Când Femeia Devine Mamă (Selfie In The Mirror: When A Woman Becomes A Mother)

Non-fiction book on motherhood. Herald Publishing House, Bucharest, Romania, 2014

## Terapie Prin Scris (Writing Therapy)

Book of essays on social and cultural subjects published on her platform ralucabarbu.ro over a period of five years. Google Play Books, 2018

Made in the USA
Monee, IL
11 May 2022